60

FARRAR
STRAUS
GIROUX

JAMES FENTON

Selected Poems

James Fenton was born in Lincoln, England, in 1949 and was educated at Magdalen College, Oxford, where he won the Newdigate Prize for Poetry. He has worked as a political journalist, drama critic, book reviewer, war correspondent, foreign correspondent and columnist. His volumes of poetry include *Terminal Moraine, The Memory of War, Children in Exile* and *Out of Danger*. His work has won him the Southern Arts Literature Award for Poetry, the Geoffrey Faber Memorial Prize and the Whitbread Award for Poetry. He is a Fellow of the Royal Society of Literature and was Oxford Professor of Poetry from 1994 to 1999. He lives in Oxford.

Selected Poems

Selected Poems

➤—◆〉•—◯•—〈◆—◄

JAMES FENTON

Farrar, Straus and Giroux / *New York*

Farrar, Straus and Giroux
19 Union Square West, New York 10003

Copyright © 2006 by Salamander Press Ltd.
All rights reserved
Distributed in Canada by Douglas & McIntyre Ltd.
Printed in the United States of America
Originally published in 2006 by Penguin Books Ltd., Great Britain
Published in the United States by Farrar, Straus and Giroux
First American edition, 2006

Library of Congress Cataloging-in-Publication Data
Fenton, James, 1949–
    {Poems. Selections}
    Selected poems / James Fenton.— 1st American ed.
        p. cm.
    ISBN-13: 978-0-374-26065-1 (pbk. : alk. paper)
    ISBN-10: 0-374-26065-6 (pbk. : alk. paper)
    I. Title

PR6056.E53 A6 2006
821′.914—dc22

                                    2006002691

Designed by Jonathan D. Lippincott

www.fsgbooks.com

1   3   5   7   9   10   8   6   4   2

Contents

Author's Note

The poems in the first two sections come from the collections *The Memory of War* (Salamander Press, 1982), *Children in Exile* (Salamander Press, 1983) and *Out of Danger* (Penguin, 1994). Many of the songs in *Out of Danger* were set to music by Dominic Muldowney in a song sequence called *Out of the East*. *The Love Bomb*, conceived originally as an opera libretto, was published in 2003 in *The Love Bomb and Other Musical Pieces* (Faber). It is due to be set to music by John Harle.

In the fourth section, "Memorial" was commissioned by the BBC for a memorial to journalists and their colleagues killed while covering wars. "Yellow Tulips" first appeared in *Areté*. "Martine's Song" and "Everything in Your Window Is a Sign" were written for *The Stare*, a film by Jay Anania. "Was That Your Idea of Love?" and "The Alibi" are part of a song sequence for Dominic Muldowney, commissioned by the BBC in connection with the Royal Philharmonic Society's Elgar Bursary.

I

FROM *The Memory of War*
AND *Children in Exile*

Wind

This is the wind, the wind in a field of corn.
Great crowds are fleeing from a major disaster
Down the long valleys, the green swaying wadis,
Down through the beautiful catastrophe of wind.

Families, tribes, nations and their livestock
Have heard something, seen something. An expectation
Or misunderstanding has swept over the hilltop
Bending the ear of the hedgerow with stories of fire and sword.

I saw a thousand years pass in two seconds.
Land was lost, languages rose and divided.
This lord went east and found safety.
His brother sought Africa and a dish of aloes.

Centuries, minutes later, one might ask
How the hilt of a sword wandered so far from the smithy.
And somewhere they will sing: "Like chaff we were borne
In the wind." This is the wind in a field of corn.

A GERMAN REQUIEM

(TO T. J. G. A.)

For as at a great distance of place, that which wee look at, appears dimme, and without distinction of the smaller parts; and as Voyces grow weak, and inarticulate: so also after great distance of time, our imagination of the Past is weak; and wee lose (for example) of Cities wee have seen, many particular Streets; and of Actions, many particular Circumstances. This *decaying sense*, when wee would express the thing it self, (I mean *fancy* it selfe,) wee call *Imagination*, as I said before: But when we would express the *decay*, and signifie that the Sense is fading, old, and past, it is called Memory. So that *Imagination* and *Memory* are but one thing . . .

—Hobbes, *Leviathan*

A German Requiem

It is not what they built. It is what they knocked down.
It is not the houses. It is the spaces between the houses.
It is not the streets that exist. It is the streets that no longer exist.
It is not your memories which haunt you.
It is not what you have written down.
It is what you have forgotten, what you must forget.
What you must go on forgetting all your life.
And with any luck oblivion should discover a ritual.
You will find out that you are not alone in the enterprise.
Yesterday the very furniture seemed to reproach you.
Today you take your place in the Widow's Shuttle.

¶

The bus is waiting at the southern gate
To take you to the city of your ancestors
Which stands on the hill opposite, with gleaming pediments,
As vivid as this charming square, your home.
Are you shy? You should be. It is almost like a wedding,
The way you clasp your flowers and give a little tug at your veil. Oh,
The hideous bridesmaids, it is natural that you should resent them
Just a little, on this first day.
But that will pass, and the cemetery is not far.
Here comes the driver, flicking a toothpick into the gutter,
His tongue still searching between his teeth.
See, he has not noticed you. No one has noticed you.
It will pass, young lady, it will pass.

¶

How comforting it is, once or twice a year,
To get together and forget the old times.
As on those special days, ladies and gentlemen,
When the boiled shirts gather at the graveside
And a leering waistcoat approaches the rostrum.
It is like a solemn pact between the survivors.
The mayor has signed it on behalf of the freemasonry.
The priest has sealed it on behalf of all the rest.
Nothing more need be said, and it is better that way—

¶

The better for the widow, that she should not live in fear of surprise,
The better for the young man, that he should move at liberty between
    the armchairs,
The better that these bent figures who flutter among the graves
Tending the night-lights and replacing the chrysanthemums
Are not ghosts,
That they shall go home.
The bus is waiting, and on the upper terraces
The workmen are dismantling the houses of the dead.

¶

But when so many had died, so many and at such speed,
There were no cities waiting for the victims.
They unscrewed the name-plates from the shattered doorways
And carried them away with the coffins.
So the squares and parks were filled with the eloquence of young
    cemeteries:
The smell of fresh earth, the improvised crosses
And all the impossible directions in brass and enamel.

¶

"Doctor Gliedschirm, skin specialist, surgeries 14–16 hours or by
    appointment."
Professor Sargnagel was buried with four degrees, two associate
    memberships
And instructions to tradesmen to use the back entrance.
Your uncle's grave informed you that he lived on the third floor, left.
You were asked please to ring, and he would come down in the lift
To which one needed a key . . .

¶

Would come down, would ever come down
With a smile like thin gruel, and never too much to say.
How he shrank through the years.
How you towered over him in the narrow cage.
How he shrinks now . . .

¶

But come. Grief must have its term? Guilt too, then.
And it seems there is no limit to the resourcefulness of recollection.
So that a man might say and think:
When the world was at its darkest,
When the black wings passed over the rooftops
(And who can divine His purposes?) even then
There was always, always a fire in this hearth.
You see this cupboard? A priest-hole!
And in that lumber-room whole generations have been housed and fed.
Oh, if I were to begin, if I were to begin to tell you
The half, the quarter, a mere smattering of what we went through!

¶

His wife nods, and a secret smile,
Like a breeze with enough strength to carry one dry leaf
Over two pavingstones, passes from chair to chair.
Even the enquirer is charmed.
He forgets to pursue the point.
It is not what he wants to know.
It is what he wants not to know.
It is not what they say.
It is what they do not say.

Cambodia

One man shall smile one day and say goodbye.
Two shall be left, two shall be left to die.

One man shall give his best advice.
Three men shall pay the price.

One man shall live, live to regret.
Four men shall meet the debt.

One man shall wake from terror to his bed.
Five men shall be dead.

One man to five. A million men to one.
And still they die. And still the war goes on.

In a Notebook

There was a river overhung with trees
With wooden houses built along its shallows
From which the morning sun drew up a haze
And the gyrations of the early swallows
Paid no attention to the gentle breeze
Which spoke discreetly from the weeping willows.
There was a jetty by the forest clearing
Where a small boat was tugging at its mooring.

And night still lingered underneath the eaves.
In the dark houseboats families were stirring
And Chinese soup was cooked on charcoal stoves.
Then one by one there came into the clearing
Mothers and daughters bowed beneath their sheaves.
The silent children gathered round me staring
And the shy soldiers setting out for battle
Asked for a cigarette and laughed a little.

From low canoes old men laid out their nets
While on the bank young boys with lines were fishing.
The wicker traps were drawn up by their floats.
The girls stood waist-deep in the river washing
Or tossed the day's rice on enamel plates
And I sat drinking bitter coffee wishing
The tide would turn to bring me to my senses
After the pleasant war and the evasive answers.

There was a river overhung with trees.
The girls stood waist-deep in the river washing,
And night still lingered underneath the eaves
While on the bank young boys with lines were fishing.
Mothers and daughters bowed beneath their sheaves
While I sat drinking bitter coffee wishing—
And the tide turned and brought me to my senses.
The pleasant war brought the unpleasant answers.

The villages are burnt, the cities void;
The morning light has left the river view;
The distant followers have been dismayed;
And I'm afraid, reading this passage now,
That everything I knew has been destroyed
By those whom I admired but never knew;
The laughing soldiers fought to their defeat
And I'm afraid most of my friends are dead.

Dead Soldiers

When His Excellency Prince Norodom Chantaraingsey
Invited me to lunch on the battlefield
I was glad of my white suit for the first time that day.
They lived well, the mad Norodoms, they had style.
The brandy and the soda arrived in crates.
Bricks of ice, tied around with raffia,
Dripped from the orderlies' handlebars.

And I remember the dazzling tablecloth
As the APCs fanned out along the road,
The dishes piled high with frogs' legs,
Pregnant turtles, their eggs boiled in the carapace,
Marsh irises in fish sauce
And inflorescence of a banana salad.

On every bottle, Napoleon Bonaparte
Pleaded for the authenticity of the spirit.
They called the empties Dead Soldiers
And rejoiced to see them pile up at our feet.

Each diner was attended by one of the other ranks
Whirling a table-napkin to keep off the flies.
It was like eating between rows of morris dancers—
Only they didn't kick.

On my left sat the Prince;
On my right, his drunken aide.
The frogs' thighs leapt into the sad purple face
Like fish to the sound of a Chinese flute.
I wanted to talk to the Prince. I wish now
I had collared his aide, who was Saloth Sar's brother.
We treated him as the club bore. He was always
Boasting of his connections, boasting with a head-shake
Or by pronouncing of some doubtful phrase.
And well might he boast. Saloth Sar, for instance,
Was Pol Pot's real name. The APCs
Fired into the sugar palms but met no resistance.

In a diary, I refer to Pol Pot's brother as the Jockey Cap.
A few weeks later, I find him "in good form
And very skeptical about Chantaraingsey."
"But one eats well there," I remark.
"So one should," says the Jockey Cap:
"The tiger always eats well,
It eats the raw flesh of the deer,
And Chantaraingsey was born in the year of the tiger.
So, did they show you the things they do
With the young refugee girls?"

And he tells me how he will one day give me the gen.
He will tell me how the Prince financed the casino
And how the casino brought Lon Nol to power.
He will tell me this.
He will tell me all these things.
All I must do is drink and listen.

In those days, I thought that when the game was up
The Prince would be far, far away—
In a limestone faubourg, on the promenade at Nice,
Reduced in circumstances but well enough provided for.
In Paris, he would hardly require his private army.
The Jockey Cap might suffice for café warfare,
And matchboxes for APCs.

But we were always wrong in these predictions.
It was a family war. Whatever happened,
The principals were obliged to attend its issue.
A few were cajoled into leaving, a few were expelled,
And there were villains enough, but none of them
Slipped away with the swag.

For the Prince was fighting Sihanouk, his nephew,
And the Jockey Cap was ranged against his brother
Of whom I remember nothing more
Than an obscure reputation for virtue.
I have been told that the Prince is still fighting
Somewhere in the Cardamoms or the Elephant Mountains.
But I doubt that the Jockey Cap would have survived his good
    connections.

I think the lunches would have done for him—
Either the lunches or the dead soldiers.

Lines for Translation into Any Language

1. I saw that the shanty town had grown over the graves and that the crowd lived among the memorials.

2. It was never very cold—a parachute slung between an angel and an urn afforded shelter for the newcomers.

3. Wooden beds were essential.

4. These people kept their supplies of gasoline in litre bottles, which their children sold at the cemetery gates.

5. That night the city was attacked with rockets.

6. The fire brigade bided its time.

7. The people dug for money beneath their beds, to pay the firemen.

8. The shanty town was destroyed, the cemetery restored.

9. Seeing a plane shot down, not far from the airport, many of the foreign community took fright.

10. The next day, they joined the queues at the gymnasium, asking to leave.

11. When the victorious army arrived, they were welcomed by the fire brigade.

12. This was the only spontaneous demonstration in their favour.

13. Other spontaneous demonstrations in their favour were organised by the victors.

Children in Exile

TO J, T, L & S

"What I am is not important, whether I live or die—
  It is the same for me, the same for you.
What we do is important. This is what I have learnt.
  It is not what we are but what we do,"

Says a child in exile, one of a family
  Once happy in its size. Now there are four
Students of calamity, graduates of famine,
  Those whom geography condemns to war,

Who have settled here perforce in a strange country,
  Who are not even certain where they are.
They have learnt much. There is much more to learn.
  Each heart bears a diploma like a scar—

A red seal, always hot, always solid,
  Stamped with the figure of an overseer,
A lethal boy who has learnt to despatch with a mattock,
  Who rules a village with sharp leaves and fear.

From five years of punishment for an offence
  It took America five years to commit
These victim-children have been released on parole.
  They will remember all of it.

They have found out: it is hard to escape from Cambodia,
    Hard to escape the justice of Pol Pot,
When they are called to report in dreams to their tormentors.
    One night is merciful, the next is not.

I hear a child moan in the next room and I see
    The nightmare spread like rain across his face
And his limbs twitch in some vestigial combat
    In some remembered place.

Oh let us not be condemned for what we are.
    It is enough to account for what we do.
Save us from the judge who says: You are your father's son,
    One of your father's crimes—your crime is you.

And save us too from that fatal geography
    Where vengeance is impossible to halt.
And save Cambodia from threatened extinction.
    Let not its history be made its fault.

They feared these woods, feared tigers, snakes and malaria.
    They thought the landscape terrible and wild.
There were ghosts under the beds in the tower room.
    A hooting owl foretold a still-born child.

And how would they survive the snows of Italy?
    For the first weeks, impervious to relief,
They huddled in dark rooms and feared the open air,
    Caught in the tight security of grief.

Fear attacked the skin and made the feet swell
  Though they were bathed in tamarind at night.
Fear would descend like a swarm of flying ants.
  It was impossible to fight.

I saw him once, doubled in pain, scratching his legs.
  This was in Pisa at the Leaning Tower.
We climbed to the next floor and his attackers vanished
  As fast as they had come. He thought some power

Some influence lurked in certain rooms and corners.
  But why was I not suffering as well?
He trod cautiously over the dead in the Campo Santo
  And saw the fading punishments of Hell

And asked whether it is true that the unjust will be tormented
  And whether those who suffer will be saved.
There are so many martyrdoms in the beautiful galleries.
  He was a connoisseur among the graves.

It was the first warm day of the year. The university
  Gossipped in friendly groups around the square.
He envied the students their marvellous education,
  Greedy for school, frantic to be in there.

On the second train he was relaxed and excited.
  For the first time he was returning home,
Pointing his pocket camera at the bright infinity of mountains.
  The winter vines shimmered like chromosomes,

Meaningless to him. The vines grew. The sap returned.
The land became familiar and green.
The brave bird-life of Italy began planning families.
It was the season of the selfish gene.

Lovers in cars defied the mad gynaecologist.
In shady lanes, and later than they should,
They were watching the fireflies' brilliant use of the hyphen
And the long dash in the darkening wood.

And then they seemed to check the car's suspension
Or test the maximum back-axle load.
I love this valley, but I often wonder why
There's always one bend extra in the road.

And what do the dogs defend behind the high wire fences?
What home needs fury on a running lead?
Why did the Prince require those yellow walls?
These private landscapes must be wealth indeed.

But you, I am glad to say, are not so fortified.
The land just peters out behind the house.
(Although, the first time the hunters came blazing through the
    garden,
  Someone screamed at me: "Get out there. What are you, man or
  mouse?")

When Duschko went mad and ate all those chickens
It was a cry for help. Now he breaks loose
And visits his fellow guards, and laughs at their misery—
Unhappy dog! So sensitive to abuse.

He thought there was a quantum of love and attention
　　Which now he would be forced to share around
As first three Vietnamese and then four Cambodians
　　Trespassed on his ground.

It doesn't work like that. It never has done.
　　Love is accommodating. It makes space.
When they were requested to abandon their home in the hayloft,
　　Even the doves retired with better grace.

They had the tower still, with its commanding eyelets.
　　The tiles were fond of them, the sky grew kind.
They watched a new provider spreading corn on the zinc tray
　　And didn't mind.

Boat people, foot people, wonky Yankee publishers—
　　They'd seen the lot. They knew who slept in which beds.
They swooped down to breakfast after a night on the tiles
　　And dropped a benediction on your heads.

And now the school bus comes honking through the valley
　　And education litters every room—
Grammars, vocabularies, the Khao-I-Dang hedge dictionary,
　　The future perfect, subjunctive moods and gloom.

So many questions in urgent need of answer:
　　What is a Pope? What is a proper noun?
Where is Milan? Who won the Second World War?
　　How many fluid ounces in a pound?

La Normandie est renommée par ses falaises et ses fromages.
What are Normandy, cliffs, cheeses and fame?
Too many words on the look-out for too many meanings.
Too many syllables for the tongue to frame.

A tiny philosopher climbs onto my knee
And sinks his loving teeth into my arm.
He has had a good dream. A friendly gun-toting Jesus
Has spent the night protecting him from harm.

He goes for Technical Lego and significant distinctions.
Suppose, he says, I have a house and car,
Money and everything, I could lose it all,
As we lost all our property in the war.

But if I have knowledge, if I know five languages,
If I have mathematics and the rest,
No one can steal that from me. The difference is:
No one inherits what I once possessed.

When I die, my education dies with me.
I cannot leave my knowledge to my son,
Says this boy in exile, and he shrugs and laughs shortly.
Whoever dreamt of Jesus with a gun?

His brother dreams all night of broken chords
And all the summer long his broken hand,
Still calloused from hard labour, figures out a prelude.
Music and maths are what he understands.

These dreams are messages. One of the dead sisters
  Says to the girl: "Do not be sad for me.
I am alive and in your twin sister's womb
  In California, as you shall see."

Some time later, the postman brings a letter from America.
  The child bride is expecting her first child.
Months afterwards, a photograph of a little girl.
  Something is reconciled.

Alone in the tower room, the twin keeps up her dancing.
  For the millionth time, Beethoven's "Für Elise"!
Little Vietnam borrows little Cambodia's toys.
  Mother America is the appeaser.

Pretending to work, I retire to the study
  And find a copy of *The Dyer's Hand*
Where I read: "An emigrant never knows what he wants,
  Only what he does not want." I understand

What it is I have seen, how simple and how powerful
  This flight, this negative ambition is
And how a girl in exile can gaze down into an olive grove
  And wonder: "Is America like this?"

For it is we, not they, who cannot forgive America,
  And it is we who travel, they who flee,
We who may choose exile, they who are forced out,
  Take to the hot roads, take to the sea,

In dangerous camps between facing armies,
    The prey of pirates, raped, plundered or drowned,
In treacherous waters, in single file through the minefields,
    Praying to stave off death till they are found,

Begging for sponsors, begging for a Third Country,
    Begging America to take them in—
It is they, it is they who put everything in hazard.
    What we do decides whether they sink or swim.

Do they know what they want? They know what they do not want.
    Better the owl before dawn than the devil by day.
Better strange food than famine, hard speech than mad labour.
    Better this quietness than that dismay.

Better ghosts under the bed than to sleep in the paddy.
    Better this frost, this blizzard than that sky.
Better a concert pianist than a corpse, an engineer than a shadow.
    Better to dance under the fresco than to die.

Better a new god with bleeding hands and feet,
    Better the painted tortures of the blest
Than the sharp leaf at the throat, the raised mattock
    And all the rest.

My dear American friends, I can't say how much it means to me
    To see this little family unfurl,
To see them relax and learn, and learn about happiness,
    The mother growing strong, the boys adept, the girl

Confident in your care. They can never forget the past.
    Let them remember, but let them not fear.
Let them find their future is delightfully accomplished
    And find perhaps America is here.

Let them come to the crest of the road when the morning is fine
    With Florence spread like honey on the plain,
Let them walk through the ghostless woods, let the guns be silent,
    The tiger never catch their eye again.

They are thriving I see. I hope they always thrive
    Whether in Italy, England or France.
Let them dream as they wish to dream. Let them dream

Of Jesus, America, maths, Lego, music and dance.

God, A Poem

A nasty surprise in a sandwich,
A drawing-pin caught in your sock,
The limpest of shakes from a hand which
You'd thought would be firm as a rock,

A serious mistake in a nightie,
A grave disappointment all round
Is all that you'll get from th'Almighty,
Is all that you'll get underground.

Oh he *said*: "If you lay off the crumpet
I'll see you alright in the end.
Just hang on until the last trumpet.
Have faith in me, chum—I'm your friend."

But if you remind him, he'll tell you:
"I'm sorry, I must have been pissed—
Though your name rings a sort of a bell. You
Should have guessed that I do not exist.

"I didn't exist at Creation,
I didn't exist at the Flood,
And I won't be around for Salvation
To sort out the sheep from the cud—

"Or whatever the phrase is. The fact is
In soteriological terms
I'm a crude existential malpractice
And you are a diet of worms.

"You're a nasty surprise in a sandwich.
You're a drawing-pin caught in my sock.
You're the limpest of shakes from a hand which
I'd have thought would be firm as a rock,

"You're a serious mistake in a nightie,
You're a grave disappointment all round—
That's all that you are," says th'Almighty,
"And that's all that you'll be underground."

The Skip

I took my life and threw it on the skip,
Reckoning the next-door neighbours wouldn't mind
If my life hitched a lift to the council tip
With their dry rot and rubble. What you find

With skips is—the whole community joins in.
Old mattresses appear, doors kind of drift
Along with all that won't fit in the bin
And what the bin-men can't be fished to shift.

I threw away my life, and there it lay
And grew quite sodden. "What a dreadful shame,"
Clucked some old bag and sucked her teeth: "The way
The young these days . . . no values . . . me, I blame . . ."

But I blamed no one. Quality control
Had loused it up, and that was that. 'Nough said.
I couldn't stick at home. I took a stroll
And passed the skip, and left my life for dead.

Without my life, the beer was just as foul,
The landlord still as filthy as his wife,
The chicken in the basket was an owl,
And no one said: "Ee, Jim-lad, whur's thee life?"

Well, I got back that night the worse for wear,
But still just capable of single vision;
Looked in the skip; my life—it wasn't there!
Some bugger'd nicked it—*without* my permission.

Okay, so I got angry and began
To shout, and woke the street. Okay. *Okay!*
And I was sick all down the neighbour's van.
And I disgraced myself on the par-*kay*.

And then . . . you know how if you've had a few
You'll wake at dawn, all healthy, like sea breezes,
Raring to go, and thinking: "Clever you!
You've got away with it." And then, oh Jesus,

It hits you. Well, that morning, just at six
I woke, got up and looked down at the skip.
There lay my life, still sodden, on the bricks;
There lay my poor old life, arse over tip.

Or was it mine? Still dressed, I went downstairs
And took a long cool look. The truth was dawning.
Someone had just exchanged my life for theirs.
Poor fool, I thought—I should have left a warning.

Some bastard saw my life and thought it nicer
Than what he had. Yet what he'd had seemed fine.
He'd never caught his fingers in the slicer
The way I'd managed in that life of mine.

His life lay glistening in the rain, neglected,
Yet still a decent, an authentic life.
Some people I can think of, I reflected
Would take that thing as soon as you'd say Knife.

It seemed a shame to miss a chance like that.
I brought the life in, dried it by the stove.
It looked so fetching, stretched out on the mat.
I tried it on. It fitted, like a glove.

And now, when some local bat drops off the twig
And new folk take the house, and pull up floors
And knock down walls and hire some kind of big
Container (say, a skip) for their old doors,

I'll watch it like a hawk, and every day
I'll make at least—oh—half a dozen trips.
I've furnished an existence in that way.
You'd not believe the things you find on skips.

II

FROM *Out of Danger*

Beauty, Danger and Dismay

Beauty, danger and dismay
Met me on the public way.
Whichever I chose, I chose dismay.

Out of Danger

Heart be kind and sign the release
As the trees their loss approve.
Learn as leaves must learn to fall
Out of danger, out of love.

What belongs to frost and thaw
Sullen winter will not harm.
What belongs to wind and rain
Is out of danger from the storm.

Jealous passion, cruel need
Betray the heart they feed upon.
But what belongs to earth and death
Is out of danger from the sun.

I was cruel, I was wrong—
Hard to say and hard to know.
You do not belong to me.
You are out of danger now—

Out of danger from the wind,
Out of danger from the wave,
Out of danger from the heart
Falling, falling out of love.

Serious

Awake, alert,
Suddenly serious in love,
You're a surprise.
I've known you long enough—
Now I can hardly meet your eyes.

It's not that I'm
Embarrassed or ashamed.
You've changed the rules
The way I'd hoped they'd change
Before I thought: hopes are for fools.

Let me walk with you.
I've got the newspapers to fetch.
I think you know
I think you have the edge
But I feel cheerful even so.

That's why I laughed.
That's why I went and kicked that stone.
I'm serious!
That's why I cartwheeled home.
This should mean something. Yes, it does.

The Ideal

This is where I came from.
I passed this way.
This should not be shameful
Or hard to say.

A self is a self.
It is not a screen.
A person should respect
What he has been.

This is my past
Which I shall not discard.
This is the ideal.
This is hard.

Hinterhof

Stay near to me and I'll stay near to you—
As near as you are dear to me will do,
    Near as the rainbow to the rain,
    The west wind to the windowpane,
As fire to the hearth, as dawn to dew.

Stay true to me and I'll stay true to you—
As true as you are new to me will do,
    New as the rainbow in the spray,
    Utterly new in every way,
New in the way that what you say is true.

Stay near to me, stay true to me. I'll stay
As near, as true to you as heart could pray.
    Heart never hoped that one might be
    Half of the things you are to me—
The dawn, the fire, the rainbow and the day.

The Possibility

The lizard on the wall, engrossed,
The sudden silence from the wood
Are telling me that I have lost
The possibility of good.

I know this flower is beautiful
And yesterday it seemed to be.
It opened like a crimson hand.
It was not beautiful to me.

I know that work is beautiful.
It is a boon. It is a good.
Unless my working were a way
Of squandering my solitude.

And solitude was beautiful
When I was sure that I was strong.
I thought it was a medium
In which to grow, but I was wrong.

The jays are swearing in the wood.
The lizard moves with ugly speed.
The flower closes like a fist.
The possibility recedes.

The Mistake

With the mistake your life goes in reverse.
Now you can see exactly what you did
Wrong yesterday and wrong the day before
And each mistake leads back to something worse

And every nuance of your hypocrisy
Towards yourself, and every excuse
Stands solidly on the perspective lines
And there is perfect visibility.

What an enlightenment. The colonnade
Rolls past on either side. You needn't move.
The statues of your errors brush your sleeve.
You watch the tale turn back—and you're dismayed.

And this dismay at this, this big mistake
Is made worse by the sight of all those who
Knew all along where these mistakes would lead—
Those frozen friends who watched the crisis break.

Why didn't they *say*? Oh, but they did indeed—
Said with a murmur when the time was wrong
Or by a mild refusal to assent
Or told you plainly but you would not heed.

Yes, you can hear them now. It hurts. It's worse
Than any sneer from any enemy.
Take this dismay. Lay claim to this mistake.
Look straight along the lines of this reverse.

I'll Explain

It's something you say at your peril.
It's something you shouldn't contain.
It's a truth for the dark and a pillow.
Turn out the light and I'll explain.

It's the obvious truth of the morning
Bitten back as the sun turns to rain,
To the rain, to the dark, to the pillow.
Turn out the light and I'll explain.

    It's what I was hoping to tell you.
    It's what I was hoping you'd guess.
    It's what I was hoping you *wouldn't* guess
    Or you wouldn't mind.
    It's a kind
    Of hopelessness.

It's the hope that you hope at your peril.
It's the hope that you fear to attain.
It's the obvious truth of the evening.
Turn out the light and I'll explain.

In Paris with You

Don't talk to me of love. I've had an earful
And I get tearful when I've downed a drink or two.
I'm one of your talking wounded.
I'm a hostage. I'm maroonded.
But I'm in Paris with you.

Yes I'm angry at the way I've been bamboozled
And resentful at the mess that I've been through.
I admit I'm on the rebound
And I don't care where are *we* bound.
I'm in Paris with you.

> Do you mind if we do *not* go to the Louvre,
> If we say sod off to sodding Notre Dame,
> If we skip the Champs Elysées
> And remain here in this sleazy
> Old hotel room
> Doing this and that
> To what and whom
> Learning who you are,
> Learning what I am.

Don't talk to me of love. Let's talk of Paris,
The little bit of Paris in our view.
There's that crack across the ceiling

And the hotel walls are peeling
And I'm in Paris with you.

Don't talk to me of love. Let's talk of Paris.
I'm in Paris with the slightest thing you do.
I'm in Paris with your eyes, your mouth,
I'm in Paris with . . . all points south.
Am I embarrassing you?
I'm in Paris with you.

The Milkfish Gatherers

TO G.L.

The sea sounds insincere
Giving and taking with one hand.
It stopped a river here last month
Filling its mouth with sand.

They drag the shallows for the milkfish fry—
Two eyes on a glass noodle, nothing more.
Roused by his vigilant young wife
The drowsy stevedore

Comes running barefoot past the swamp
To meet a load of wood.
The yellow peaked cap, the patched pink shorts
Seem to be all his worldly goods.

The nipa booths along the coast
Protect the milkfish gatherers' rights.
Nothing goes unobserved. My good custodian
Sprawls in the deckchair through the night.

Take care, he says, take care—
Not everybody is a friend.
And so he makes my life more private still—
A privacy on which he will attend.

But the dogs are sly with the garbage
And the cats ruthless, even with sliced bread,
As the terns are ruthless among the shoals.
Men watch the terns, then give the boat its head

Dragging a wide arc through the blue,
Trailing their lines,
Cutting the engine out
At the first sign.

A hundred feet away
Something of value struggles not to die.
It will sell for a dollar a kilo.
It weighs two kilos on the line—a prize.

And the hull fills with a fortune
And the improbable colours of the sea
But the spine lives when the brain dies
In a convulsive misery.

Rummagers of inlets, scourers of the deep,
Dynamite men, their bottles crammed with wicks,
They named the sea's inhabitants with style—
The slapped vagina fish, the horse's dick.

Polillo "melts" means it is far away—
The smoking island plumed from slash and burn.
And from its shore, busy with hermit crabs,
Look to Luzon. Infanta melts in turn.

The setting sun behind the Sierra Madre
Projects a sharp blue line across the sky
And in the eastern glow beyond Polillo
It looks as if another sun might rise—

As if there were no night,
Only a brother evening and a dawn.
No night! No death! How could these people live?
How could the pressure lanterns lure the prawns?

Nothing of value has arrived all day—
No timber, no rattan. Now after dark,
The news comes from the sea. They crowd the beach
And prime a lantern, waiting for the shark.

The young receive the gills, which they will cook.
The massive liver wallows on the shore
And the shark's teeth look like a row of sharks
Advancing along a jaw.

Alone again by spirit light
I notice something happening on a post.
Something has burst its skin and now it hangs,
Hangs for dear life onto its fine brown ghost.

Clinging exhausted to its former self,
Its head flung back as if to watch the moon,
The blue-green veins pulsing along its wings,
The thing unwraps itself, but falls too soon.

The ants are tiny and their work is swift—
The insect-shark is washed up on their land—
While the sea sounds insincere,
Giving and taking with one hand.

At dawn along the seashore come
The milkfish gatherers, human fry.
A white polythene bowl
Is what you need to sort the milkfish by.

For a hatched fish is a pair of eyes—
There is nothing more to see.
But the spine lives when the brain dies
In a convulsive misery.

Jerusalem

I

Stone cries to stone,

   Heart to heart, heart to stone,

And the interrogation will not die

   For there is no eternal city

   And there is no pity

And there is nothing underneath the sky

   No rainbow and no guarantee—

There is no covenant between your God and me.

II

It is superb in the air.

Suffering is everywhere

And each man wears his suffering like a skin.

   My history is proud.

   Mine is not allowed.

This is the cistern where all wars begin,

   The laughter from the armoured car.

This is the man who won't believe you're what you are.

III

This is your fault.

This is a crusader vault.

The Brook of Kidron flows from Mea She'arim.

   I will pray for you.

I will tell you what to do.
I'll stone you. I shall break your every limb.
Oh I am not afraid of you
But maybe I should fear the things you make me do.

IV

This is not Golgotha.
This is the Holy Sepulchre,
The Emperor Hadrian's temple to a love
Which he did not much share.
Golgotha could be anywhere.
Jerusalem itself is on the move.
It leaps and leaps from hill to hill
And as it makes its way it also makes its will.

V

The city was sacked.
Jordan was driven back.
The pious Christians burned the Jews alive.
This is a minaret.
I'm not finished yet.
We're waiting for reinforcements to arrive.
What was your mother's real name?
Would it be safe today to go to Bethlehem?

VI

This is the Garden Tomb.
No, *this* is the Garden Tomb.
I'm an Armenian. I am a Copt.
This is Utopia.
I came here from Ethiopia.

This hole is where the flying carpet dropped
The Prophet off to pray one night
And from here one hour later he resumed his flight.

VII

Who packed your bag?
I packed my bag.
Where was your uncle's mother's sister born?
Have you ever met an Arab?
Yes I am a scarab.
I am a worm. I am a thing of scorn.
I cry Impure from street to street
And see my degradation in the eyes I meet.

VIII

I am your enemy.
This is Gethsemane.
The broken graves look to the Temple Mount.
Tell me now, tell me when
When shall we all rise again?
Shall I be first in the great body count?
When shall the tribes be gathered in?
When, tell me, when shall the Last Things begin?

IX

You are in error.
This is terror.
This is your banishment. This land is mine.
This is what you earn.
This is the Law of No Return.
This is the sour dough, this the sweet wine.

This is my history, this my race
And this unhappy man threw acid in my face.

                    X
Stone cries to stone,
    Heart to heart, heart to stone.
These are the warrior archaeologists.
    This is us and that is them.
    This is Jerusalem.
These are the dying men with tattooed wrists.
    Do this and I'll destroy your home.
I have destroyed your home. You have destroyed my home.

December 1988

For Andrew Wood

What would the dead want from us
Watching from their cave?
Would they have us forever howling?
Would they have us rave
Or disfigure ourselves, or be strangled
Like some ancient emperor's slave?

None of my dead friends were emperors
With such exorbitant tastes
And none of them were so vengeful
As to have all their friends waste
Waste quite away in sorrow
Disfigured and defaced.

I think the dead would want us
To weep for what *they* have lost.
I think that our luck in continuing
Is what would affect them most.
But time would find them generous
And less self-engrossed.

And time would find them generous
As they used to be
And what else would they want from us
But an honoured place in our memory,

A favourite room, a hallowed chair,
Privilege and celebrity?

And so the dead might cease to grieve
And we might make amends
And there might be a pact between
Dead friends and living friends.
What our dead friends would want from us
Would be such living friends.

Out of the East

Out of the South came Famine.
Out of the West came Strife.
Out of the North came a storm cone
And out of the East came a warrior wind
And it struck you like a knife.
Out of the East there shone a sun
As the blood rose on the day
And it shone on the work of the warrior wind
And it shone on the heart
And it shone on the soul
And they called the sun—Dismay.

And it's a far cry from the jungle
To the city of Phnom Penh
And many try
And many die
Before they can see their homes again
And it's a far cry from the paddy track
To the palace of the King
And many go
Before they know
It's a far cry.
It's a war cry.
Cry for the war that can do this thing.

A foreign soldier came to me
And he gave me a gun
And he predicted victory
Before the year was done.

He taught me how to kill a man.
He taught me how to try.
But he forgot to say to me
How an honest man should die.

He taught me how to kill a man
Who was my enemy
But never how to kill a man
Who'd been a friend to me.

You fought the way a hero fights—
You had no head for fear
My friend, but you are wounded now
And I'm not allowed to leave you here

Alive.

Out of the East came Anger
And it walked a dusty road
And it stopped when it came to a river bank
And it pitched a camp
And it gazed across
To where the city stood
When
Out of the West came thunder
But it came without a sound
For it came at the speed of the warrior wind

And it fell on the heart
And it fell on the soul
And it shook the battleground

And it's a far cry from the cockpit
To the foxhole in the clay
And we were a
Coordinate
In a foreign land
Far away
And it's a far cry from the paddy track
To the palace of the King
And many try
And they ask why
It's a far cry.
It's a war cry.
Cry for the war that can do this thing.

Next year the army came for me
And I was sick and thin
And they put a weapon in our hands
And they told us we would win

And they feasted us for seven days
And they slaughtered a hundred cattle
And we sang our songs of victory
And the glory of the battle

And they sent us down the dusty roads
In the stillness of the night
And when the city heard from us
It burst in a flower of light.

The tracer bullets found us out.
The guns were never wrong
And the gunship said Regret Regret
The words of your victory song.

Out of the North came an army
And it was clad in black
And out of the South came a gun crew
With a hundred shells
And a howitzer
And we walked in black along the paddy track
When
Out of the West came napalm
And it tumbled from the blue
And it spread at the speed of the warrior wind
And it clung to the heart
And it clung to the soul
As napalm is designed to do

And it's a far cry from the fireside
To the fire that finds you there
In the foxhole
By the temple gate
The fire that finds you everywhere
And it's a far cry from the paddy track
To the palace of the King
And many try
And they ask why
It's a far cry.
It's a war cry.
Cry for the war that can do this thing.

My third year in the army
I was sixteen years old
And I had learnt enough, my friend,
To believe what I was told

And I was told that we would take
The city of Phnom Penh
And they slaughtered all the cows we had
And they feasted us again

And at last we were given river mines
And we blocked the great Mekong
And now we trained our rockets on
The landing-strip at Pochentong.

The city lay within our grasp.
We only had to wait.
We only had to hold the line
By the foxhole, by the temple gate

When
Out of the West came clusterbombs
And they burst in a hundred shards
And every shard was a new bomb
And it burst again
Upon our men
As they gasped for breath in the temple yard.
Out of the West came a new bomb
And it sucked away the air
And it sucked at the heart
And it sucked at the soul
And it found a lot of children there

And it's a far cry from the temple yard
To the map of the general staff
From the grease pen to the gasping men
To the wind that blows the soul like chaff
And it's a far cry from the paddy track
To the palace of the King
And many go
Before they know
It's a far cry.
It's a war cry.
Cry for the war that has done this thing.

A foreign soldier came to me
And he gave me a gun
And the liar spoke of victory
Before the year was done.

What would I want with victory
In the city of Phnom Penh?
Punish the city! Punish the people!
What would I want but punishment?

We have brought the King home to his palace.
We shall leave him there to weep
And we'll go back along the paddy track
For we have promises to keep.

For the promise made in the foxhole,
For the oath in the temple yard,
For the friend I killed on the battlefield
I shall make that punishment hard.

Out of the South came Famine.
Out of the West came Strife.
Out of the North came a storm cone
And out of the East came a warrior wind
And it struck you like a knife.
Out of the East there shone a sun
As the blood rose on the day
And it shone on the work of the warrior wind
And it shone on the heart
And it shone on the soul
And they called the sun Dismay, my friend,
They called the sun—Dismay.

Blood and Lead

Listen to what they did.
Don't listen to what they said.
What was written in blood
Has been set up in lead.

Lead tears the heart.
Lead tears the brain.
What was written in blood
Has been set up again.

The heart is a drum.
The drum has a snare.
The snare is in the blood.
The blood is in the air.

Listen to what they did.
Listen to what's to come.
Listen to the blood.
Listen to the drum.

The Ballad of the Imam and the Shah
An Old Persian Legend

TO C.E.H.

It started with a stabbing at a well
Below the minarets of Isfahan.
The widow took her son to see them kill
The officer who'd murdered her old man.
The child looked up and saw the hangman's work—
The man who'd killed his father swinging high.
The mother said: "My child, now be at peace.
The wolf has had the fruits of all his crime."

From felony to felony to crime
From robbery to robbery to loss
From calumny to calumny to spite
From rivalry to rivalry to zeal

All this was many centuries ago—
The kind of thing that couldn't happen now—
When Persia was the empire of the Shah
And many were the furrows on his brow.
The peacock the symbol of his throne
And many were its jewels and its eyes
And many were the prisons in the land
And many were the torturers and spies.

From tyranny to tyranny to war
From dynasty to dynasty to hate

From villainy to villainy to death
From policy to policy to grave

The child grew up a clever sort of chap
And he became a mullah, like his dad—
Spent many years in exile and disgrace
Because he told the world the Shah was bad.
"Believe in God," he said, "believe in me.
Believe me when I tell you who I am.
Now chop the arm of wickedness away.
Hear what I say. I am the great Imam."

From heresy to heresy to fire
From clerisy to clerisy to fear
From litany to litany to sword
From fallacy to fallacy to wrong

And so the Shah was forced to flee abroad.
The Imam was the ruler in his place.
He started killing everyone he could
To make up for the years of his disgrace.
And when there were no enemies at home
He sent his men to Babylon to fight.
And when he'd lost an army in that way
He knew what God was telling him was right.

From poverty to poverty to wrath
From agony to agony to doubt
From malady to malady to shame
From misery to misery to fight

He sent the little children out to war.
They went out with his portrait in their hands.
The desert and the marshes filled with blood.
The mothers heard the news in Isfahan.
Now Babylon is buried under dirt.
Persepolis is peeping through the sand.
The child who saw his father's killer killed
Has slaughtered half the children in the land.

From felony
to robbery
to calumny
to rivalry
to tyranny
to dynasty
to villainy
to policy
to heresy
to clerisy
to litany
to fallacy
to poverty
to agony
to malady
to misery—

The song is yours. Arrange it as you will.
Remember where each word fits in the line
And every combination will be true
And every permutation will be fine:

From policy to felony to fear
From litany to heresy to fire
From villainy to tyranny to war
From tyranny to dynasty to shame

From poverty to malady to grave
From malady to agony to spite
From agony to misery to hate
From misery to policy to fight!

I Saw a Child

I saw a child with silver hair.
Stick with me and I'll take you there.
    Clutch my hand.
    Don't let go.
The fields are mined and the wind blows cold.
The wind blows through his silver hair.

The Blue Vein River is broad and deep.
The branches creak and the shadows leap.
    Clutch my hand.
    Stick to the path.
The fields are mined and the moon is bright.
I saw a child who will never sleep.

Far from the wisdom of the brain
I saw a child grow old in pain.
    Clutch my hand.
    Stay with me.
The fields are mined by the enemy.
Tell me we may be friends again.

Far from the wisdom of the blood
I saw a child reach from the mud.
    Clutch my hand.
    Clutch my heart.

The fields are mined and the moon is dark.
The Blue Vein River is in full flood.

Far from the wisdom of the heart
I saw a child being torn apart.
  Is this you?
  Is this me?
The fields are mined and the night is long.
Stick with me when the shooting starts.

Tiananmen

Tiananmen
Is broad and clean
And you can't tell
Where the dead have been
And you can't tell
What happened then
And you can't speak
Of Tiananmen.

You must not speak.
You must not think.
You must not dip
Your brush in ink.
You must not say
What happened then,
What happened there
In Tiananmen.

The cruel men
Are old and deaf
Ready to kill
But short of breath
And they will die
Like other men
And they'll lie in state
In Tiananmen.

They lie in state.
They lie in style.
Another lie's
Thrown on the pile,
Thrown on the pile
By the cruel men
To cleanse the blood
From Tiananmen.

Truth is a secret.
Keep it dark.
Keep it dark
In your heart of hearts.
Keep it dark
Till you know when
Truth may return
To Tiananmen.

Tiananmen
Is broad and clean
And you can't tell
Where the dead have been
And you can't tell
When they'll come again.
They'll come again
To Tiananmen.

Hong Kong, June 15, 1989

The Ballad of the Shrieking Man

A shrieking man stood in the square
And he harangued the smart café
In which a bowlered codger sat
A-twirling of a fine moustache
A-drinking of a fine Tokay

And it was Monday and the town
Was working in a kind of peace
Excepting where the shrieking man
A-waving of his tattered limbs
Glared at the codger's trouser-crease

Saying

Coffee's mad
And tea is mad
And so are gums and teeth and lips.
The horror ships that ply the seas
The horror tongues that plough the teeth
The coat
The tie
The trouser clips
The purple sergeant with the bugger-grips
Will string you up with all their art
And laugh their socks off as you blow apart.

The codger seeming not to hear
Winked at the waiter, paid the bill
And walked the main street out of town
Beyond the school, beyond the works
Where the shrieking man pursued him still

And there the town beneath them lay
And there the desperate river ran.
The codger smiled a purple smile.
A finger sliced his waistcoat ope
And he rounded on the shrieking man

Saying

Tramps are mad
And truth is mad
And so are trees and trunks and tracks.
The horror maps have played us true.
The horror moon that slits the clouds
The gun
The goon
The burlap sacks
The purple waistcoats of the natterjacks
Have done their bit as you can see
To prise the madness from our sanity.

On Wednesday when the day was young
Two shrieking men came into town
And stopped before the smart café
In which another codger sat
Twirling his whiskers with a frown

And as they shrieked and slapped their knees
The codger's toes began to prance
Within the stitching of their caps
Which opened like a set of jaws
And forced him out to join the dance

Saying

Arms are mad
And legs are mad
And all the spaces in between.
The horror spleen that bursts its sack
The horror purple as it lunges through
The lung
The bung
The jumping-bean
The I-think-you-know-what-you-think-I-mean
Are up in arms against the state
And all the body will disintegrate.

On Saturday the town was full
As people strolled in seeming peace
Until three shrieking men appeared
And danced before the smart café
And laughed and jeered and slapped their knees

And there a hundred codgers sat.
A hundred Adam's apples rose
And rubbed against their collar studs
Until the music came in thuds
And all the men were on their toes

Saying

Hearts are mad
And minds are mad
And bats are moons and moons are bats.
The horror cats that leap the tiles
The horror slates that catch the wind
The lice
The meat
The burning ghats
The children buried in the butter vats
The steeple crashing through the bedroom roof
Will be your answer if you need a proof.

The codgers poured into the square
And soon their song was on all lips
And all did dance and slap their knees
Until a horseman came in view—
The sergeant with the bugger-grips!

He drew his cutlass, held it high
And brought it down on hand and head
And ears were lopped and limbs were chopped
And still the sergeant slashed and slew
Until the codger crew lay dead

Saying

God is mad
And I am mad
And I am God and you are me.
The horror peace that boils the sight

The horror God turning out the light.
The Christ
Who killed
The medlar tree
Is planning much the same for you and me
And here's a taste of what's in store—
Come back again if you should want some more.

On Sunday as they hosed the streets
I went as usual to pray
And cooled my fingers at the stoup
And when the wafer touched my tongue
I thought about that fine Tokay

And so I crossed the empty square
And met the waiter with a wink
A-sweeping up of severed heads
A-piling up of bowler hats
And he muttered as he poured my drink

Saying

Waiting's mad
And stating's mad
And understating's mad as hell.
The undertakings we have made
The wonder breaking from the sky
The pin
The pen
The poisoned well
The purple sergeant with the nitrate smell
Have won their way and while we wait

The horror ships have passed the straits—
The vice
The vine
The strangler fig
The fault of thinking small and acting big
Have primed the bomb and pulled the pin
And we're all together when the roof falls in!

Fireflies of the Sea

Dip your hand in the water.
Watch the current shine.
See the blaze trail from your fingers,
Trail from your fingers,
Trail from mine.
There are fireflies on the island
And they cluster in one tree
And in the coral shallows
There are fireflies of the sea.

Look at the stars reflected
Now the sea is calm
And the phosphorus exploding,
Flashing like a starburst
When you stretch your arm.
When you reach down in the water
It's like reaching up to a tree,
To a tree clustered with fireflies,
Fireflies of the sea.

Dip your hand in the water.
Watch the current shine.
See the blaze trail from your fingers,
Trail from your fingers,
Trail from mine

As you reach down in the water,
As you turn away from me,
As you gaze down at the coral
And the fireflies of the sea.

Cut-Throat Christ

or the New Ballad of the Dosi Pares

Oh the Emperor sat on an ivory throne
And his wives were fat and all their jewels shone
And the Emperor said: It's plain to see
Christ was an emperor just like me.

Well the rich have a Christ and he's nobody's fool
And he pays for their kids to go to convent school
And their momma drives them home to tea.
She says: Christ is a rich bitch just like me.

But *I* say:

I say he sold his body to some foreign queer
And he sold his blood for just a case of beer
And he sold his soul to the fraternity.
Christ became a cut-throat just like me.

There's a Christ for a whore and a Christ for a punk
A Christ for a pickpocket and a drunk
There's a Christ for every sinner but one thing there aint—
There aint no Christ for any cutprice saint.

Well I was casting for fish by the North Harbour Pier
When this guy called Jesus says to me: Come here—
If you want to join the fraternity,
Lay down your nets and you can follow me.

So I left my nets and I left my line
And I followed my Jesus to the Quiapo shrine
And he told me many stories of his enemy—
It was General Ching of the EPD.

And I swore to the Black Nazarene there and then
I'd go out and kill one of the General's men
And when I brought my *beinte-nuebe* for the boss to see
That guy called Jesus he was proud of me.

Oh the Emperor sat on an ivory throne.
He had twelve brave peers and he loved each one.
We were twelve disciples and our strength was proved
But I was the disciple whom Jesus loved.

There's a Christ for a whore and a Christ for a punk
A Christ for a pickpocket and a drunk
There's a Christ for every sinner but one thing there aint—
There aint no Christ for any cutprice saint.

Well Jesus was a drinker as you might expect.
We got through plenty stainless and a few long necks
And then Jesus got mad as mad can be.
He said: One of you punks is gonna squeal on me.

Now that General Ching has put a price on my head
With disciples like you I'm as good as dead—
There's one who will betray me to the EPD.
We said: Tell me boss, tell me boss, is it me?

But there wasn't the leisure and there wasn't the time
To find out from Jesus who would do this crime

For a shot rang out and we had to flee
From General Ching and half the military.

Oh the Emperor sat on an ivory throne
And out of twelve brave peers there was just one bad one
And Christ had twelve disciples and they loved him so
But one out of twelve is just the way things go.

There's a Christ for a whore and a Christ for a punk
A Christ for a pickpocket and a drunk
There's a Christ for every sinner but one thing there aint—
There aint no Christ for any cutprice saint.

Well I ran like crazy and I ran like fuck
And for the next three days I did my best to duck
And then I made my way back to the EPD.
I said: The General said he had a job for me.

Well the General he saw me and his face grew grim.
He said: Watch it guys, don't stand too close to him—
That's our old friend Judas and he wants his fee,
But the guy called Jesus he is roaming free.

I said: What's the deal? He said: We killed him, sure,
We filled him full of what we had and then some more,
We dumped him back in Tondo for his momma to see
And now he's resurrected with a one, two, three.

I said: General Ching, if what you say is true
I'm gonna need some protection out of you.
He said: Just pay him off now and let me be—
We don't protect a mediocrity.

'Cos the Emperor sat on an ivory throne
But that was long ago and now the Emperor's gone
And this guy called Jesus he is something new:
You crucify him once and he comes back for you.

We've dumped him in the Pasig, we've thrown him in the Bay,
We've nixed him in the cogon by the Superhighway,
We've chopped him into pieces and we've spread him around
But three days later he is safe and he is sound.

There's a Christ for a whore and a Christ for a punk
A Christ for a pickpocket and a drunk
There's a Christ for every sinner but one thing there aint—
There aint no Christ for any cutprice saint.

Now Manila's not the place for a defenceless thing—
You either go with Jesus or with General Ching
And I'd been with both and after what I'd been
I knew my only hope was the Black Nazarene.

So I go barefoot down to Quiapo and the streets are packed
And they're carrying the Nazarene on their backs
And just one step and it's plain to see
That Christ will crush them to eternity—

The Christ of the Aztecs, the Juggernaut God,
The Christ of the Thorn and the Christ of the Rod
And they're carrying the Christ along two lengths of rope
'Cos the Cut-Throat Christ's a cut-throat's only hope

And there's the man who killed the Carmelites, the Tad-tad gang,
The man who sells the ArmaLites in Alabang

And General Ching, the EPD, the senatorial bets,
The twelve disciples and the drum majorettes,

The Emperor Charlemagne, the rich bitch and the queer,
The guy called Jesus by the North Harbour Pier
And they're coming down to Quiapo and they've all made a vow
To wipe the sweat from the Black Nazarene's brow.

Oh the Emperor sat on an ivory throne
But in a cut-throat world a man is on his own
And what I've got is what you see—
Cut-Throat Christ, don't turn your back on me.

Gabriel

I come home to the cottage.
I climb the balcony.
It's the archangel Gabriel
Waiting there for me.

He says: Boss, boss, cut the loss,
Don't take on so.
Don't get mad with Gabriel.
Let it go.

I go into the kitchen
To fix myself a drink.
It's the archangel Gabriel
Weeping by the sink.

He says: Boss, boss, cut the loss,
Don't take on so.
Don't get mad with Gabriel.
Let it go.

I say: You've been away in Magsaysay,
You've not clocked in all week;
You're as strong as an ox,
But you're work-shy
With your head bowed low and your pleading eyes
And I'm too mad to speak.

I come home two hours later.
The archangel drops a tear.
He's sitting there in the same old chair
And he's drunk all the beer.

He says: Boss, boss, cut the loss,
Don't take on so.
Don't get mad with Gabriel.
Let it go.

I say: You've drunk yourself into outer space.
You're giving me one of those looks.
You're as wild as the moon in storm time
And I'd like to know the reason I'm
Supposed to keep you on the books.

Yes I should have known when I took you on
When you tumbled from the sky
That you're set in your ways and that's all.
You're a Gabriel and you've had a fall.
You can't change and nor can I
Gabriel
You can't change and nor can I.

The Ballad of the Birds

There's a mynah bird a-squawking
In the ipil-ipil tree.
I say: What do you want,
What do you want,
What do you want from me?
For my crops have all been planted
And the rainy season's here
But the baby in the hammock
Will not see out the year

And it goes

Crack crack
I'll be back
I'll be back like a heart attack
I'll be back when your hopes are wrecked
I'll be back when you most expect

There's a turtle dove a-weeping
In the crest of the dap-dap tree.
I say: What do you want,
What do you want,
What do you want from me?
For my son has gone to Saudi
And my daughter's in the States

But I'll have to borrow money
And I can't afford the rate

And it goes

Coo coo
Hard on you
Crack crack
I'll be back
I'll be back like a heart attack
I'll be back when your hopes are wrecked
I'll be back when you most expect

And the kingfisher goes shrieking
At the edge of the shining sea.
I say: What do you want,
What do you want,
What do you want from me?
For my wife has gone to the graveyard
To clear the weeds away
And the rains have failed and the land is dry
And there'll be some grief today

And it goes

Kraa kraa
Life is hard
Coo coo
Hard on you
Crack crack
I'll be back
I'll be back like a heart attack

I'll be back when your hopes are wrecked
I'll be back when you most expect

There are sparrows in the paddy
On the road to the cemetery.
I say: What do you want,
What do you want,
What do you want from me?
There's a grief that knocks you senseless.
There's a grief that drives you wild.
It picks you up.
It throws you down.
It grabs your hair.
It throws you in the air.
At the coffin of a child

And it goes

Peep peep
A child comes cheap
Kraa kraa
Life is hard
Coo coo
Hard on you
Crack crack
I'll be back
I'll be back like a heart attack
I'll be back when your hopes are wrecked
I'll be back when you most expect

Oh I'm nothing but a farmer
In the harvest of the year

And the rains have failed
And the land is sold
And I'm left in grief and fear
And there's a carrion crow alighting
On the crest of the banyan tree.
I say: What do you want,
What do you want,
What in the name of God do you want from me?

I Know What I'm Missing

It's a birdcall from the treeline.
I hear it every day.
It's the loveliest of the songbirds
And I'm glad it comes this way
And I stop to listen
And forget what I've to do
And I know what I'm missing—
My friend
My friend.

It's fluttering in the palm fronds
With a flash of black and gold.
It's the whistling of the oriole
And its beauty turns me cold
And I stop to listen
And forget what I've to do
And I know what I'm missing—
My friend
My friend.

Do you wonder if I'll remember?
Do you wonder where I'll be?
I'll be home again next winter
And I hope you'll write to me.
When the branches glisten
And the frost is on the avenue

I'll know what I'm missing—
My friend
My friend
I'm missing you.

Here Come the Drum Majorettes!

There's a girl with a fist full of fingers.
There's a man with a fist full of fivers.
There's a thrill in a step as it lingers.
There's a chance for a pair of salivas—

For the

Same hat
Same shoes
Same giddy widow on a sunshine cruise
Same deck
Same time
Same disappointment in a gin-and-lime

It's the same chalk on the blackboard!
It's the same cheese on the sideboard!
It's the same cat on the boardwalk!
It's the same broad on the catwalk!

There's a Gleb on a steppe in a dacha.
There's a Glob on a dig on the slack side.
There's a Glubb in the sand (he's a pasha).
There's a glib gammaglob in your backside

Saying

Gleb meet Glubb.

Glubb meet Glob.

God that's glum, that glib Glob dig.

"Dig that bog!"

"Frag that frog."

"Stap that chap, he snuck that cig."

It's the same ice on the racetrack!

It's the same track through the pack ice!

It's the same brick in the ice pack!

It's the same trick with an ice pick!

There's a thing you can pull with your eyeballs.

There's a tin you can pour for a bullshot.

There's a can you can shoot for a bullseye.

There's a man you can score who's an eyesore.

I'm an

Eyesore.

You're the thing itself.

You've a

Price or

You'd be on the shelf.

I'm a loner

In a lonesome town—

Barcelona—

It can get you down.

It's the same scare with a crowbar!

It's the same crow on the barstool!

It's the same stool for the scarecrow!

It's the same bar!

Ho!

Ha!

Like a spark from the stack of a liner
Like a twig in the hands of a dowser
With the force of the fist of a miner
(With the grace and the speed of a trouser)

In a

Blue moon
In a blue lagoon
She's got blue blue bloomers in a blue monsoon.

Wearing blue boots
And a blue zoot suit
He's a cruising bruiser with a shooter and a cute little
Twin blade
Sin trade
In a
Blue brown
New Town.

It's the same hand on the windpipe!
It's the same sand in the windsock!
It's the same brand on the handbag!
It's the same gland in the handjob!

The room is black.
The knuckles crack.
The blind masseuse walks up your back.

The saxophone
Is on its own
Pouring out the *Côtes du Rhône.*

When you're down to your last pair of piastres.
When you're down on your luck down in Przemyśl,
When your life is a chain of disasters
And your death you believe would be sameish,

When the goat has gone off with the gander
Or the goose with the grebe or the grouper
Then—a drum majorette—you can stand her:
She's a brick—she's a gas—she's a trouper

Saying

Jane meet John.
John meet Jane.
Take those jimjams off again
Jezebel.
Just as well.
Join the jive with Jules and June.
Geoffrey, Jesus, Jason, Jim,
Jenny, Jilly, Golly Gee—
If it's the same for you and him
It's the same for you and me:

It's the same grin on the loanshark!
It's the same goon in the sharkskin!
It's the same shark in the skin-game!
It's the same game
Same same

It's the same old rope for to skip with!
It's the same Old Nick for to sup with
        With a long spoon
        To the wrong tune

And it's hard for a heart to put up with!

The Orange Dove of Fiji

TO R. & B. O'H.

On the slopes of Taveuni
The Barking Pigeons woof
But when I saw the Orange Dove
I nearly hit the roof

And would have surely had there been
A roof around to hit
But the roofs of Taveuni
Are down on the lower bit

While up there in the forest
The Silktails have survived
Where they "forage in the substage"
And you feel you have *arrived*

As an amateur ornithologist
In the midst of a silktail flock
Until you hear behind you
A "penetrating tock"

And you find six feet above your head
What you were looking for—
The Orange Dove of Fiji,
No less, no more.

The female of the Orange Dove
Is actually green.
The really orange *male* Orange Dove
Is the one you've seen.

It must have been dipped in Day-Glo
Held by its bright green head.
The colour is preposterous.
You want to drop down dead.

It turns around upon its perch
Displaying all the bits
That are mentioned in Dick Watling's book
And the description fits.

Then it says: "Tock—okay, is that
Enough to convince you yet?
Because that, my friend, is all tock tock
That you are going to get."

Oh the Many-Coloured Fruit Dove
Is pretty enough to boot
And I'm afraid the purple swamphen
Looks queerer than a coot

Like a flagrant English Bishop
Let loose among his flock
With brand-new orange gaiters
(And that's just the swamphen cock)

But the Orange Dove is something
Spectacular to see
So I hope they don't fell another single
Taveuni tree.

The Exchange

I met the Muse of Censorship
And she had packed her bags
And all the folk of Moscow
Were hanging out the flags.

I asked her what her prospects were
And whither her thoughts did range.
She said: "I am off to Dublin town
On a cultural exchange.

"And folk there be in Cambridge
Who like the way I think
And there be folk in Nottingham
Whom I shall drown in ink

"And when we reach America
The majorettes will sing:
Here comes the Muse of Censorship—
This is a very good thing."

I went to the Finland Station
To wave the Muse goodbye
And on another platform
A crowd I did espy.

I saw the Muse of Freedom
Alighting from the train.
Far from that crowd I wept aloud
For to see that Muse again.

An Indistinct Inscription Near Kom Ombo
(Meroitic Cursive)

I was born to a kiss and a smile.
I was born to the hopes of a prince.
I dipped my pen in the Nile
And it hasn't functioned since.

III

The Love Bomb

THE LOVE BOMB
A musical drama

If any man come to me, and hate not his father, and mother, and wife and children, and brethren, and sisters, yea, and his own life also, he cannot be my disciple.

—Luke 14:26

Dramatis Personae

Martin
Anna
John
Brother Paul, a cult leader
Brother Simon, an elder of the cult
Police officer
Male and female cult members
Police and firemen

ACT ONE

SCENE ONE

At a pub table.
Martin and John.

JOHN:

    I'm not objective.

    I've told you that before.

    I've got my own perspective

    And it's the opposite of yours

    And I mistrust myself

    And I mistrust my motives overall

    But Anna has left you, Martin,

    She's left you for Brother Paul.

MARTIN:

    You think she's having an affair.

JOHN:

    No more than all the rest of them.

    It's like a harem over there.

    They worship him

    And they'll do anything at all

    To efface themselves

    To abase themselves

    To embrace their Brother Paul.

MARTIN:

I feel I ought to follow her
As if she'd gone out for a walk
And simply failed to reappear.
Even as we talk
I feel a panic coming on.
I feel that I've no business to be here.
I should be looking for her.
I should be raising the alarm.
I should be out there with a torch
In case she's come to any harm.

JOHN:

What makes you think
She'd thank you for your pains?
She's run away.
She's run away and slammed the church door in your face.

MARTIN:

You've always hated her.

JOHN:

No, but I was jealous once.
I'm not objective, as you know.

{They part.}

1. Love and Be Silent

JOHN [*solus*]:

"Love and be silent":
That was a good idea,

A harsh resolve,
A chilly way to start the year.

Frosty philosophy,
Cold comfort for the heart.
Suffer to some purpose.
Let the bleeding start.

SCENE TWO

In a sitting-room.
Martin and Anna.

MARTIN:

I know if it's over it's over.
I don't want to speak about us.
But you know how your father and mother—
You know how they fuss.
You know they get worried. They wonder
If it's something they've said or they've done.
They feel you're becoming a stranger.
And they don't know what's wrong.

ANNA:

Who doesn't know?

MARTIN:

Your mother. Your father.

ANNA:

    Who is my father?

    Who is my mother?

MARTIN:

    Anna!

ANNA:

    What do you mean:

    "If it's all over"?

MARTIN:

    I said I didn't want

    To bring that up again.

    It isn't why I'm here.

ANNA:

    Why are you here?

    Why are you here, Martin?

    Who sent you here?

MARTIN:

    Nobody sent me here.

    Anna!

2. Speak to Me

Speak to me, Anna, like you used to do.

Speak to me once again.

Speak to me just this once, even though we're through.

Try to explain.

It may not help. It may not tide me over
This drift, this deadness where you used to be.
But there's a way of letting down a lover.
Let me down more tenderly.

And there's a way of letting down a lover
Without this dreadful slamming of the door.
And I have friends who, after it was over,
Have become friends once more—

Live in the same place, hang around together,
And know each other's partners, and they don't fight.
And some—you wouldn't know they'd once been lovers.
It's water under the bridge. And that's all right.

It's water under the bridge. It's only normal.
It's a case of that was then and this is now.
But when I stare down from the bridge at all that water
It doesn't seem to make the blindest bit of sense, somehow.

ANNA:
　　I've been busy.

MARTIN:
　　You don't have to lie to me!

ANNA:
　　No, it's more than busy.
　　It's like being loved for the first time
　　And being able to love in return.
　　It's like having a family
　　Where there was none before.

MARTIN:

>Anna!

ANNA:

>You asked me to tell you
>And I'm telling you.
>It's like
>Who is my father?
>Who is my mother?
>And suddenly the answer comes in a flash.

MARTIN:

>My father is Brother Paul.
>My mother is Brother Paul.
>My aunt and uncle
>My sister and my brother—
>Everyone is Brother Paul.

ANNA:

>You don't have to yell.
>You asked me and I'm telling you.
>Listen to me, Martin.

3. Love and Death

>You know what London is like.
>Sometimes you wonder why you bother—
>Getting up, getting ready,
>Going through the rigmarole
>As if you were dressing a paper doll:
>This is Anna's underwear.

These are her shoes.
This is her office outfit—
Skirt and blouse and matching bag
Held in place by paper tabs.

Anna is going to work.
This is Anna at the bus-stop.
Here comes Anna's bus.
Oh look.
Anna didn't get on the bus.
What's happened?
Maybe Anna is going crazy.
Maybe Anna's lost her mind.

Don't go down that street, Anna.
Don't go down that street.
That's where all the murderers live.
Well, maybe it's a murderer I want to meet.

Don't go down the towpath, Anna.
Don't go along the canal.
That's where all the accidents happen.
Treat me to an accident. Be my pal.

  'Cos one door opens on love
  And one door opens on death.
  And one door opens on the lift shaft.
  Turn the handle. Hold your breath.

Don't go out at night, Anna.
Don't go out in the dark.
That's when all the skeletons

Rattle their bones
Rattle their bones
And drag you down to Davy Jones.
Well, maybe Davy Jones would be quite a lark.

'Cos one door opens on love
And one door opens on death
And one door opens on the lift shaft
On the lift shaft
On the lift shaft
Turn the handle, hold your breath
Death or love
Love or death
Every door means death or love.

MARTIN:

You scare me.
You scare me when you talk like that.

ANNA:

Maybe I scare myself.
Maybe we *should* be scared
When we look into our souls.

MARTIN:

Is that what they've been teaching you?

ANNA:

Is that what they've been teaching you?
Is that what they've been preaching at you?
No, it's something I've learned for myself.
Come with me.
Come with me to Brother Paul.

A church in a converted cinema.
Dancers and Singers.

4. He Is the Beat

CHORUS:

    Beat, meditation, dance and light.
    Beat, meditation, dance and light.
    He is the light.
    He is the beat,
    The runway on the funway to the one-way street.
    [I said]
    Beat, meditation, dance and light.
    Beat, meditation, dance and light.
    He is the way.
    He is the truth,
    The saviour on the wavelength with the emphasis on youth.
    The emphasis on youth.
    The emphasis on truth.
    The saviour on the wavelength with the emphasis on youth.
    [I said]
    Beat, meditation, dance and light.
    Beat, meditation, dance and light.
    Dance to the beat.
    It comes from the street.
    Liberation, Salvation is a one-way street.
    There's no turning back.
    There's no turning slack.
    There's no turning back 'cos it's a one-way street,

A runway,
A funway,
A one-way street.

5. Magic Hands

GUITARIST (BROTHER SIMON):
You walk the stony places.
You walk fair and tall.
Along the lonely ridges
You hear the ravens call.
But always there is Someone
To catch you when you fall.

Magic hands
Will catch you when you fall.
Oo oo.
Magic hands
Will catch you when you fall.

You ride the lonely canyon.
You go for many a day
Forlorn but not forsaken.
Your sorrow makes you stray.
But always there is Someone
To wipe your tears away.

Magic hands
Will wipe those tears away.
Aa aa.
Magic hands
Will wipe those tears away.

And some are born to falter
And some are born to fail
And some are born to stumble
Along the darkening trail

Along the darkening trail, O Lord,
Along the darkening trail,
There's many you will find, My Lord,
Along the darkening trail.

You walk the stony places.
You go through many lands.
You cross the frozen river.
You cross the parching sands.
And no one sees that Someone.
No one sees those magic hands.

Magic hands
No one sees those magic hands
Oh Lord.
Magic hands
No one sees those magic hands.

6. Christ Is My Idea of Glamour

CHORUS:

Christ is my idea of glamour.
Christ is where I want to be.
Though I squint and though I stammer
Christ will make a star of me.

By his birth and by his passion,
By his suffering in the end,
Only Christ can set the fashion.
Only Christ can set the trend.
Amen.

ANNOUNCER (BROTHER SIMON):

Ladies and gentlemen, I give you, the man you've all
been waiting for—the one and only Brother Paul.

> *{Dry ice. Lights. Brother Paul is dressed in white suit, black
> shirt and dark glasses.}*

7. Coming Together

BROTHER PAUL:

Coming together in love
Coming together in hope
Coming together in ecstasy
That's what coming together should be.

Love is a draught of fire
Hope will fan the flame
Fan the flame of ecstasy
That's what coming together should be.

Coming together in sin
Burning our sins away
Burning our sins in ecstasy
That's what coming together should be.

I am a man of sin
You are the children of God
We are the children of ecstasy
That's what coming together should be.

Coming together with fire
Fire and wind and flame
Burning our shame in ecstasy
Coming together with you, with me.

Coming together with God
Coming together with me
Coming together with ecstasy
You in God and God in me.

I am a man of God
I am a man of flame
I am a man of ecstasy
I am a man with God in me!

8. Turn

CHORUS:

Turn from the cradle, turn from the hearth,
Turn from your house and home,
Turn to the love, turn to the wrath,
Turn to the terror to come.

Turn from your father, turn from his hand,
Turn from his cuffs and blows,

Turn to the God who will smite the land
With a thousand, thousand more than those.

Will you pause at the threshold, hesitate
When you hear your mother cry?
Turn to the plague, turn to the scourge,
Turn to the blood that is in the sky.

Turn to the streaming, streaming blood,
Turn to the terror to come,
Turn to the plague, the famine and the flood,
The flood which will wash away your home.

This is the flood. This is the wrath.
This is the hovering dove.
These are the flames of ecstasy.
This is the terror of love.

9. The Insect Sermon

BROTHER PAUL:

And we are the insects in the sight of God.
And we are insects.
Every saint was an insect.
Every apostle too.

When I was a child
I collected insects
And pinned them to a balsa-wood board
And I killed them with a chloroform swab.

Christ was an insect
Just like us
And they took him
And pinned him to a board

And Christ flapped his wings
Just as my insects used to do
And the vinegar in the sponge
Was the chloroform swab

And he pressed his nose into the sponge
And he breathed in the vinegar
He breathed in the vinegar
Of the father who hated him

But had sent him this vinegar
This vinegar of mercy.
And he said Why?
Why have you forsaken me?

Does every father hate his son?
Does every son look up one day
As Isaac looked up
And saw his father Abraham with his knife—

The knife raised high,
The son pinned down
On the balsa-wood board,
The insect ready to die?

How could our father Abraham
Find strength to pierce his son like an insect

Unless a kind of hatred
Slumbered in his heart?

And God said: Search out
And find that hatred for your son,
That insect of yours—
Search out that hatred for your insect son.

And Abraham said to the Lord:
Where, Lord, where shall I find it?
And the Lord said:
There, where your love is, there you will find your hatred.

And Isaac looked up
And he saw that his father Abraham had found the hatred,
Had found the hatred slumbering in his love
And Isaac knew he was an insect, no more than a vinegar flea.

As Christ breathed in the chloroform,
As Christ breathed in the vinegar mingled with gall,
He knew he was an insect in the sight of God
As we are insects in the sight of God.

This is the mystery of love.
This is the mystery slumbering in God's love.

10. Farewell

CHORUS:
Farewell to the love of the world.
Farewell to the love of our home.

Farewell to the love of our family.
Farewell to the love of our friends.

I am turning my face to the fire.
I am turning my face to the flood.
I am turning my face to the love and wrath,
To the love and wrath of God.

Oh burn me in your fire.
Oh drown me in your flood.
Consume me in the love and wrath,
In the love, in the wrath of God.

SCENE FOUR

At a pub table again.
Martin and John.

JOHN:

Well, then, she's lost it.
She's gone mad for Brother Paul.

MARTIN:

Don't say that.

JOHN:

She has signed away her sanity
And she wants you to do the same.

MARTIN:

She wanted me to go along
And see for myself.
And her parents wanted me to.

JOHN:

Her parents?
I thought you and Anna were through.
What's all this about her parents?
What are they to you?

MARTIN:

They simply asked me.
They wanted me to rescue her.

JOHN:

Rescue her? Rescue?
Rescue her from what she wants to do?
Rescue her from deserting you?
Rescue her from hurting you?
What is this foolishness?
Can you not see?
They want you to save their family.
And she—
Maybe she doesn't know
What there is in store
But maybe she wants to hurt you
Just a little more.

11. Let's Go Over It All Again

Some people are like that.
They split up and then they think:
Hey, maybe we haven't hurt each other to the uttermost.
Let's meet up and have a drink.

Let's go over it all again.
Let's rake over the dirt.
Let me pick that scab of yours.
Does it hurt?

Let's go over what went wrong—
How and why and when.
Let's go over what went wrong
Again and again.

We hurt each other badly once.
We said a lot of nasty stuff.
But lately I've been thinking how
I didn't hurt you enough.

Maybe there's more where that came from,
Something more malign.
Let me damage you again
For auld lang syne.
Yes, let me see you bleed again
For auld lang syne.

MARTIN:

John, I can't let Anna drop.
I almost feel I've pushed her into this.

JOHN *{handing Martin a file of clippings}*:

I've brought you the cuttings you asked for.

Here they are.

You'll see what Brother Paul is like.

Once you join you never leave.

Once you join it's goodbye dad,

Goodbye mum.

Goodbye pounds.

Goodbye pence.

Goodbye soul.

Goodbye sense.

They say that salvation is a one-way street

And they mean what they say.

They have their methods. That's why you seldom meet

Anyone who got away.

{They get up to leave the pub.}

12. I'm Not Objective

Listen to me.

If you have to go with Anna

There's nothing I can do.

Maybe you have to try at least.

I could be wrong.

And I admit that I have selfish reasons too—

Reasons to regret her hold over you.

I'm not objective.

I've seen you suffering too long.

It drives me nuts.
I feel the blade
Twist in my guts.

I'm not objective.
I've watched her take you up
And put you through the mangle
And that outrages me.
And that's—well—that's a sort of angle.

It made me feel for you
Far in excess of what I should.
It made your suffering real for me—
Perhaps too real for my own good.
I can't conceal from you
I'm not objective, I've a point of view.

Don't sign your soul away, Martin.
Don't sign your soul away.

END OF ACT ONE

ACT TWO

SCENE ONE

The church as before.
Brother Paul, Martin, Anna, cult members.

13. You Are the Rock

BROTHER PAUL:

When Jesus came to gather his disciples
Down by the snoring lake of Galilee
D'you think his folk were happy to lose their Simon,
To say farewell to the sons of Zebedee?

Zebedee wept and tore his hair and garments
And smeared his face with ashes from the hearth
And Simon's mother screamed among the potsherds
When Simon followed Jesus down the path.

Zebedee wept to see his sons desert him
For he was frail and getting on in years.
Soon he'd be left with nobody to help him
And so he cursed his offspring through his tears.

And Simon followed Jesus to the lakeside
And still his mother screamed and called him home.

And Jesus said to Simon: Thou art Peter
And Peter shalt thou die for me in Rome.

You are the Rock. They are the Sons of Thunder,
No longer now the Sons of Zebedee
And you shall leave your mothers and your brothers
Beside the snoring lake of Galilee.

CHORUS:

We are the Rock. We are the Sons of Thunder.
And we have turned our backs on hearth and home.
We are the saints and we shall soon be martyrs
In Ephesus, Jerusalem and Rome.

BROTHER PAUL:

Now Mary called her other sons together
And she had grown so thin and pale and sad.
She told her boys to take control of Jesus
For Jesus had undoubtedly gone mad.

And so his brothers sent a line to Jesus
To tell him they would wait for him outside
But Jesus knew that they had come to get him
And this is how the Son of Man replied.

He said:

Who is my mother? Who is my brother?
Who is my sister? I am alone.
These are my followers and my believers
And this is all the family I own.

This is the Rock. He is my mother.
These are the Sons of Thunder. They're my kin.
These are my sisters. These are my brothers.
And this is where my mission will begin.

CHORUS:

We are the Rock. We are the Sons of Thunder.
And we have turned our backs on hearth and home.
We are the saints and we shall soon be martyrs
In Ephesus, Jerusalem and Rome.

BROTHER PAUL:

Martin, you have been with us all this time.
Now you must tell us how you find us.
Now you must share your feelings with us.

14. The Love Bomb

MARTIN:

It's just as Anna promised me.
It's exactly as she said.
So many friends and so much love.
It's like a love bomb in my head.

It's like a love bomb in the brain.
It's like a love bomb in the heart,
Blowing all my past away,
Blowing my old life apart.

The happiness I once enjoyed
Seems such a small, a trivial thing.

The friendships and the family
Seem so remote and posturing.

It's like a putting into port.
It's like a stepping off a train,
Like an embrace and like a dream,
Like finding something lost again.

Like finding that a wall is false
And watching as the panel slides
And stepping into a hidden space
And finding what the panel hides:

The hidden life, the hidden love,
The looming trees, the brilliant lawn
Reflected in the looking-glass,
The garden at the break of dawn.

BROTHER PAUL:

> Well, it is true that we have given you
> All the love we can
> And yet I sometimes wonder . . .

MARTIN:

> What do you wonder?

BROTHER PAUL:

> I wonder what you are holding back.
> I wonder why you find it
> So hard to give,
> So easy to receive.

MARTIN:

But I have given you all my love.

BROTHER PAUL:

All your love?
Was that *all* your love, Martin?
I thought I saw
Through a chink in the door
Another room, another love,
A love that you were holding in reserve
In case this love turned sour on you.

I thought I saw another love,
A love perhaps from long ago,
A different love, perhaps a secret love,
Hoarded and treasured in the soul,
In case this love walked out on you,
In case it turned its back on you,
As certain loves are liable to do.

Oh—"I have given you all my love"—
"All my love" trips easily off the tongue.
Judas Iscariot gave Jesus all his love
But still he held some back
Just in case.

MARTIN:

Brother Paul!

BROTHER PAUL:

I see the comparison offends you.
But it is true.

Judas Iscariot loved Jesus once
Enough to leave his family and home.
But still he kept a little in reserve,
A little pot of coins he buried in a cave.

MARTIN:

If it's a matter of money—

BROTHER PAUL:

It's not the money.
It's the meaning of the money.
It's not the little pot of coins.
It's the meaning of the little pot of coins.

MARTIN:

You think I would betray you,
Brother Paul?

BROTHER PAUL:

Someone will betray me, Martin,
That much is certain.
Someone who loves me will betray me.
Why should it not be you?
When first you loved Anna,
Did you not betray a friend?

MARTIN:

Anna!

ANNA:

It is true.
John loved you, and you betrayed him.

You loved John, and you betrayed him.
And sometimes as we lay in bed together
Sometimes when we were making love
I thought: how easy you found it, this betrayal.
If you betrayed John, why should you not betray me?

MARTIN:

I never betrayed you.

ANNA:

Maybe you're betraying me now.
Maybe you're betraying all of us.

Why did you follow me, Martin?
Why did you follow me here?
Was it the love of Jesus?
Or was it something less sincere?

Who was it who put you up to it?
Who set you on my tail?

MARTIN:

Wait, it was *you* invited me.

ANNA:

I don't remember it like that.
I remember you hated Brother Paul.
Why would I invite you?
Somebody sent you.
That's what I've always felt about you.
Somebody sent you to keep an eye on me
To spy on me.

Who sent you here, Martin?
Who sent you here?

MARTIN:

Nobody sent me here.
Your father and mother were worried about you,
But nobody—

ANNA:

My father and mother:
You're working for my father and mother.
You are spying on me,
Spying on us,
Spying on Brother Paul.

MARTIN:

It's not spying.
I came here out of concern.

BROTHER PAUL:

So everything you said just now
Was a lie.

MARTIN:

What do you mean?

BROTHER PAUL:

About the love you had found
And the love you had given—
It was all a lie.

MARTIN:

No. I was surprised.

I—

Look, if you don't want me here,

I shall go.

BROTHER PAUL:

Go? Just like that?

You are not going anywhere

Until we find out who you are working for.

MARTIN:

You can't do that to me.

I am free to go any time I want.

{The male acolytes move to block the doors.}

It's a free country.

I can go any time I want.

BROTHER PAUL:

Who are you working for, Martin?

Who are you working for?

ANNA:

Judas Iscariot!

Judas Iscariot!

CHORUS:

Judas, Judas, Judas.

MARTIN:

It's a free country.

I can walk out the door.

You can't stop me.

{In a panic, he makes to go.}

BROTHER PAUL:

Deal with him now.

Deal with him.

{The men overpower Martin, and knock him out with a chloroform swab.}

SCENE TWO

At the country house headquarters of the cult.
Martin is being held in a basement cell.
We can hear the cult members, off-stage, practising a hymn.
A male orderly brings in a tray of food, while another keeps watch at the door.

MARTIN:

Where am I?

How long have I been here?

Will nobody speak to me?

{The orderly leaves the room, without acknowledging Martin's presence.}

But I *know* where I am.
I know where I must be.
Sometimes a car goes by
And I can hear the gravel on the drive.

The sound of someone raking leaves,
Scraping the ground . . . the mopping of a floor,
The hasty steps along a corridor—
The noises of a grand estate.

At dawn, somewhere nearby
An airport opens its runways to the sky.

I should be honoured after all
To be the guest of Brother Paul,
To be invited to his country place.
But it doesn't feel like an honour.
It feels like a sore head after a bad fall,
A catastrophic fall from grace.

15. The Vapour Trail

Now through the grating of my cell
I look up at a strip of autumn sky
And often, chalked across the blue,
There's a vapour trail,
A vapour trail . . .
And then, I don't know why,
John, my dear friend,
I start to think of you.

Dawn brings these planes from distant lands,
Red-eyed tycoons from far-flung ports of call.
Dawn lifts the luggage through the flaps
Onto the carousel
The carousel
And wakes the baggage hall.
Dawn will bring you, perhaps.

Perhaps that vapour trail is where
Your plane passed over me here in my jail.
That line is the trajectory
Of your breakfast tray,
Your breakfast tray.
Perhaps that is your trail
And you look down on me.

Look down on me, my friend, look down
And think of me now as I think of you
And think of us as we were then
From your vapour trail,
Your vapour trail . . .
Your line of chalk on blue.
Think well of me again,
    My friend—
    Whatever hurt I may have done,
    For I intended none.
    Forgive the hurt that I did not intend
    And let it mend.
Think well of me again.

{Enter Brother Simon.}

Who are you?

BROTHER SIMON:

I am Brother Simon, your advocate.

MARTIN:

A lawyer?

BROTHER SIMON:

Not exactly.
It is my job to plead for you
With Brother Paul
And I have to tell you
The case looks bad.

MARTIN:

How so?

BROTHER SIMON:

Anna and the brethren searched your flat.
They found these cuttings in a file
And they found these letters
From a man called John.
Who is this John?

MARTIN:

A friend.

BROTHER SIMON:

More than a friend, I think.

MARTIN:

What business is it of yours?

BROTHER SIMON:

I told you.
I am your advocate,
The only friend who can help you out of this.
We have to know
Why you were spying on us.
You were working for John.
The cuttings file proves that.
But who is John?
And why is he working against us?
You have to tell us this.
You have to tell us everything.

MARTIN:

And if I refuse?

BROTHER SIMON:

To refuse is to say:
I am still working against you,
Working against God's will,
Working against Brother Paul.
Is that the message you wish to send?

MARTIN:

No.

BROTHER SIMON:

John was your lover, was he not?

{Brother Simon places a tape-recorder on the table, and turns it on.}

MARTIN:

John was my lover.

BROTHER SIMON:

And would be still,
If he could have his way.

MARTIN:

And would be still, perhaps,
If Anna had not had her way.

BROTHER SIMON:

That sounds bitter.

MARTIN:

I've no right to be bitter.
It was I who walked out on John.
Why did you say "And would be still"?

BROTHER SIMON:

There was a recent letter in your flat.

MARTIN:

May I read it?

{Brother Simon hands him the letter.}

John, solus.

16. You've Disappeared from the Screen

JOHN:

Where are you, Martin? Where have you been?
Like some night-flying long-haul jet from JFK,
You've disappeared from the screen.
I'm almost ashamed
The number of messages I've left
On your machine.
You've disappeared from the screen.

You've disappeared from the screen.
One moment you were there and we were talking.
Next thing I knew
You'd vanished in the blue.
Now when I try to phone I feel I'm stalking.
Arrest me, do.
Arrest me for pestering you.
We used to be inseparable.
Have I done something irreparable?
Am I suddenly unclean?
You've disappeared from the screen.

You've disappeared from the screen.
The Archway bus was asking after you.
And Clissold Crescent
Looked thoroughly unpleasant

The last time I came wandering idly through
And gave a glance
At your unwatered plants—
The trailing petunias
Looked frail and impecunious.
I could not intervene.
You've disappeared from the screen.

I'm not a monk.
I've been out once or twice,
Got a bit drunk
And met somebody nice
But I knew all the time
I'd never find
What I was thinking of—
Something a little less like sex
And more like making love
Something profound for a change—
Something better than those nefarious gymnastics
With coked-up blokes in various elastics—
That was never my scene.
You've disappeared from the screen.

You've disappeared from the screen.
And London seems so meaninglessly leafy
And all the men
Irrelevant again—
The tall, the small, the epicene, the beefy.
I'm stuck without you.
I'm out of luck without you.
Consider it from *my* angle
In your Bermuda Triangle.

Is it nice or is it mean
That you've disappeared from the screen?

In the main hall of the cult's country headquarters.
The elaborate interior suggests a nineteenth-century stately pile,
which has been fitted out to form a kind of throne-room. The cult
members, men and women placed apart, stand in formation
around the throne, which will be occupied by Brother Paul.
Brother Paul, Brother Simon, Martin, Anna, cult members.

17. Chorus: Oh Sing the Song of Moses

CHORUS:

Oh sing the song of Moses,
The song of the Son of Man.
He comes to reap his harvest,
His sickle is in his hand.

He reaches for the cluster
And finds the time is good.
High as a horse's bridle
There flows the river of blood.

It floweth from the winepress,
The winepress of his ire.
It floweth from the winepress
To the sea of glass and fire.

And we are clothed in linen
And our harps are in our hands
And we shall see the Seven Plagues
Visited on the land.

And we shall hear the trumpets
And we shall hear the drums.
We shall be girdled all in gold
When Armageddon comes.

BROTHER SIMON:

    I bring to the Tent of Testimony
    A penitent sinner.

BROTHER PAUL:

    Is he truly a penitent?

BROTHER SIMON:

    I have examined him
    And do believe so.

BROTHER PAUL:

    Martin, you have been examined
    And found a penitent.
    Kneel before me and bow the head.

18. Worship Me

    God says:

    Not until you worship me,
    Worship me,

Worship me,
Not until you worship me
Shall the soul of sin be free.

Worship is empty of design.
Worship is empty of desire.
Worship is an emptying.
Worship is a cleansing fire.

Worship me. I am the wind.
Worship me. I am the rain.
Worship me. I am the fire—
The fire upon the darkening plain.

Worship me. I am the word.
Worship me. I am the breath.
Worship me. I am the life.
Worship me. I am the death.

I am the death in Golgotha.
I am the death upon the tree.
I am the tomb. I am the shroud.
I am the body. Worship me.

END OF ACT TWO

ACT THREE

SCENE ONE

In John's Archway flat, London.
John is making coffee for Martin.

MARTIN:

Good old Archway.
I never thought I'd live to say
The words.
It sounds absurd.
But often when they kept me in that cell
I thought of you,
I thought of us—
I thought of hopping on the Archway bus
Back then, when we got on so well—

JOHN:

Milk?

MARTIN:

And Archway seemed the dullest of all dumps—

JOHN:

One lump or two?

MARTIN:

You don't buy sugar lumps!

JOHN:

You don't know what I do.
You forget—
You've been away.
You've been away for a year and a day
Without so much as a by-your-leave.

{Seriously}

So now they trust you again.
They've let you out on parole.

MARTIN:

Now I'm a man on a mission.
I have to trap a human soul.

JOHN:

To trap a particular soul
Or will any soul do?

MARTIN:

To trap a very particular soul—
They've ordered me to come back with you.

{John laughs.}

JOHN:

Dead or alive!
I'm flattered. But I decline.

What could they want with me?
They know that I detest the lot of them.
They know that I'm the enemy.

MARTIN:

They think that I've a power over you.

JOHN:

Now then, in that they may be right.

MARTIN:

And Brother Paul—he has a way with him
When he gets someone in his sights.
I'm scared of him.
The more I see his plan unfold
The warier I become of him.
There's something cold,
Something akin to murder in his eyes
But it's a murder that he offers you
As if it were a prize,
As if you were supposed to say:
Yes, murder my soul,
Murder my soul and make my day.

JOHN:

Get out now, while you can.

MARTIN:

I want to.
There's only one thing stopping me.

JOHN:

Anna.

MARTIN:

It's not quite Anna anymore.

It's more the promise that I made.

It's like a pride in finishing a job.

I'd like to take her back home and then

I'd cheerfully never see Anna again.

JOHN:

Is this a labour of love

Or a labour of hate?

19. If I Left Her There

MARTIN:

If I left her there,

I'd feel that I had left her there to die.

There's a pestilence in there.

They're doomed.

You only have to look them in the eye.

It's like an endgame.

It's like they're staring at the sky

Searching for a sign

Searching for the line:

The End Is Nigh.

JOHN:

They're dangerous

And what you are doing is dangerous,

Dangerous for you,
Which makes it dangerous for me.

If I went back there with you
I would contact the police first
And tell them what I was going to do.
I'd take no chances with Brother Paul.

SCENE TWO

*Back at the cult headquarters, where the windows in the great
hall have been covered with wire grilles. A table has been set up
beside the throne, on which a large punchbowl has been placed.
Martin, John, Brother Paul, Brother Simon, Anna, cult
members.*

20. Christ Was Crucified in Sodom

CHORUS:

    Christ was crucified in Sodom
    And the corpses lined the streets
    And the Sodomites made merry
    Cracking nuts and swapping sweets.

    And the corpses lay unburied
    Three whole days and three whole nights
    For the corpses were the prophets
    Who had lashed the Sodomites.

163

They were men who came in sackcloth
And their mouths were full of fire
And they shut the skies of Heaven
With their wisdom and their ire.

They were men who came in sackcloth
Through the fire and through the flood
And they spread a plague in Sodom
And the water turned to blood.

So no rain could fall on Sodom
While the prophets prophesied
Till a beast came up from Hades,
Fought the prophets, and they died.

Came the cloud and came the thunder
And the cisterns filled with rain
And the Sodomites were dancing
In the Cities of the Plain.

Came the thunder, came the lightning,
Came a voice from Heaven that cried:
Come up here, my slaughtered prophets,
To the wound that is in my side.

To the wound and to the wisdom
To the welt and to the weal,
Come up here, my slaughtered prophets,
And the Lamb shall break the seal.

Came the lightning, came the earthquake
And the prophets rose on high

And the Sodomites were slaughtered
In the ruins where they lie.

Christ was crucified in Egypt.
Pharaoh laughed to see him die.
Christ was crucified in Sodom
And they mocked his agony.

This is Egypt. This is Sodom.
Listen to the thunder peal.
We are saints and we are prophets
And the Lamb shall break the seal.

BROTHER PAUL:
　　Step forward, John.

　　Friends, this is John,
　　The friend of Martin,
　　Anna's friend.

　　I saw John in a dream
　　And I said: John, John,
　　Why do you persecute me?
　　Why do you long to destroy what you could love?
　　When you see a rose, do you tear it to pieces?
　　When you see a kingfisher, do you reach for a gun?
　　Pity the rose. Pity the kingfisher.

　　And John said to me:
　　Paul, Paul,
　　Does the rose ask mercy of the whirlwind?
　　Does the kingfisher cry to the eagle:

Pity me, I am a kingfisher?
Does the fire forgive the granary?
Does the flood spare the villages of the plain?

The scorpion says: I am a scorpion.
The tiger says: I am a tiger.
Only man is a riddle.

And I said to John in my dream:
Tiger and scorpion, eagle and whirlwind,
Fire and flood, what is your name?

And he told me the number of the letters of his name.
He told me the number of the letters of his name.

JOHN {*interrupting*}:
And you awoke. And it was all a dream.

And you awoke, Brother Paul, and it was all a dream.
The revelation was a dream.

And you awoke to a world
In which there was a man whose name you knew
Who despised you with all his heart.
And you thought:
I shall invite him to that temple of mine,
That prison-temple where I lock up my worshippers
And maybe he will worship me
Or maybe I shall deal with him.

I see that all the windows are barred
And all the doors bolted.

They are not barred against burglars.
They are barred to keep your worshippers in.
Worship me or else, the windows say.
What kind of temple is that?
What kind of worship is that?

I see a table set with a great bowl—
A sort of loving cup.
What sort of love is in the bowl, Brother Paul?
What sort of potion?
There is death in the bowl.
There is poison in the bowl.

And what is this I smell on the air?
There is petrol on the air.
There is murder and conflagration on the air.
You are a murderer, Brother Paul.
First you murder the soul,
Then you murder the body.
Then you plan a conflagration—
As if the fire will absolve you.

BROTHER PAUL:
Deal with him, Brother Simon.
Deal with the Antichrist.

> *{At this exact moment, the great windows of the hall are lit up
> by searchlights, and there are blue flashing lights outside. Brother
> Simon hesitates.}*

POLICE:

Open up. Open up.

Brother Paul, we have a warrant for your arrest

For false imprisonment.

BROTHER PAUL:

Brother Simon, set fire to the fuses.

Set fire to the fuses.

Let the Last Things begin!

{Brother Simon goes up the great stairs, and starts to set light to the upper floor. The police begin knocking the door down and breaking the lower windows. As they do so, the Chorus are singing in the background, while they begin taking the poison.}

21. Farewell (reprise)

CHORUS:

Farewell to the love of the world.

Farewell to the love of our home.

Farewell to the love of our family.

Farewell to the love of our friends.

I am turning my face to the fire.

I am turning my face to the flood.

I am turning my face to the love and wrath,

To the love and wrath of God.

Oh burn me in your fire.

Oh drown me in your flood.

Consume me in the love and wrath,

In the love, in the wrath of God.

MARTIN:

    Anna,

    Come with us now

    Before it is too late.

ANNA:

    Let go of me,

    Antichrist, Antichrist.

    You and your Satan-lover John,

    You and my mother are poison to me,

    You and my father are poison to me,

    Poison to me,

    Poison to me,

    You and your lover are poison to me.

MARTIN:

    Anna, don't—

    {Anna is dousing herself with petrol.}

ANNA:

    I am turning my face to the fire!

    I am turning my face to the fire!

    {She is engulfed.}

BROTHER PAUL:

    Anna has chosen the Way.

    Anna has chosen the Cup.

    Anna has chosen the Call.

MARTIN:

Go poison yourself,

Go poison yourself, Brother Paul.

Poison yourself.

You poisoned my life long ago.

Poison yourself.

Make sure you do it well.

Drink long, drink deep and drink yourself to Hell.

BROTHER PAUL:

Antichrist, I drink to you!

{Brother Paul drinks the poison.
The police break in and rush Martin and John out of the
collapsing house.}

SCENE THREE

In front of the burning remains of the house.
Police and firemen at work in the background.
John and Martin.

JOHN:

Martin—

MARTIN:

Don't tell me I did everything I could!

Don't tell me that.

I don't want to hear.

I don't want sympathy.

JOHN:

    I wasn't going to offer sympathy.

    I was going to say

    The officer said

    They would let us go home soon.

    Where will you go?

MARTIN:

    Where will I go?

    How do *I* know where I'll go?

    Oh, leave me alone.

    Leave me alone.

       {Martin solus.}

MARTIN:

    It's true I don't know where I'll go

    Or what I'll do.

    How strange this is

    And how horrible

    As if she'd hung a piece of carrion around my neck

    And said: wear that, wear it forever,

    Wear this death of mine around your neck.

    I can't face my flat.

    Her fingerprints are all over it.

    She turned the whole place upside down

    Looking for evidence against me.

    How thoroughly she hated me.

    How thoroughly she hates me still

    Alone in her circle of Hell.

    Oh I can feel her hating me.

{John and the Officer.}

JOHN:

Officer,

I'm worried for my friend.

He shouldn't be left alone tonight.

Not after seeing Anna go like that.

I'm afraid he'll do something stupid.

OFFICER:

Could you put him up?

JOHN:

Of course.

OFFICER:

Why don't you speak to him?

JOHN:

I've tried.

Maybe he'll listen to you.

Tell him he mustn't be alone tonight.

OFFICER:

I'll see what I can do.

{Officer and Martin.}

OFFICER:

You've a place to go tonight?

MARTIN:

Yes.

OFFICER:

Anyone there?

{Martin is silent.}

You know you shouldn't be alone tonight.
You've had a shock. You've had a scare.
There's a delayed reaction
In cases such as this
And I should feel responsible
If anything should come amiss.

MARTIN:

You think I might kill myself?

OFFICER:

The strangest people do.
But I should just feel happier
With someone looking after you.

MARTIN:

Well, if I did do something,
I'd be entitled.

OFFICER *{sharply}*:

Oh, you'd be entitled.
You know what I wish
More than anything in the world?
I wish, when young lads like you

String yourselves up,
You'd spare a thought for the likes of us—
The ones who have to cut you down.
Do you think we don't wake screaming in the night?
Do you think we forget your faces?
Do you think you're entitled to haunt us
For the rest of your lives?

> *{Martin hides his face.*
> *The Officer continues mildly, after a pause.}*

Your friend seems kind.
He's got a level head.
I asked him if he'd mind
Offering you a bed.

MARTIN:

What did he say?

OFFICER:

He's got a spare bed.
He's happy to put you up.

MARTIN:

He said that?

OFFICER:

Talk to him yourself.
I'll fetch the driver.

> *{John and Martin.}*

22. Let It Mean Everything

MARTIN:

The officer said
You had a bed for me.

JOHN:

It's true.
Don't you remember?

MARTIN:

Yes, I remember our old bed.
But I'm afraid
If I come back with you
What it would mean.

JOHN:

Let it mean nothing.
Let it mean
The night was cold—
We shared a bed.
A cold night calls for company.

MARTIN:

I could have done that once,
Not now.
Not after all I've put you through.
If I go back with you
It would have to mean everything.

JOHN:

Well then,
Let it mean everything.
I'm on for that as well.
I'm on for "everything,"
Martin.
Can't you tell?

Let it mean everything.
Give everything a go.
I'll settle for everything.
I'd gamble everything on just one throw.

MARTIN:

It would have to mean everything.
It would mean that I was coming back again for good.
It would mean that we were starting again,
Starting from scratch—

JOHN:

What's wrong with that? Perhaps we could.

MARTIN:

It would have to mean everything.
It would have to mean everything.

{With a sudden vehemence}

And I can't do it.
I mustn't go back.
Leave me alone, John!
For God's sake leave me alone!

{The officers return and open the car doors.}

OFFICER:

Okay gentlemen,
We're taking you back to London.
Where do you want dropping off?

JOHN:

Archway for me.

OFFICER:

And what about Martin here?
Archway for you?

{Martin is silent.}

Now remember what I said.
I should feel responsible.
You don't want me to feel responsible, do you?

MARTIN:

No, you are right.
I don't want you to—
I don't want anyone to feel responsible.

John, does your offer still stand?

{John is silent.
Martin becomes agitated.}

John?
Does your offer still stand?

JOHN *{with mild exasperation, after a pause}*:
What do you think?

MARTIN:
I think the night is cold
And a cold night calls for company.

JOHN *{laughing}*:
That was the password.
You've remembered the password!

OFFICER *{to the driver}*:
We'll be dropping these two gentleman at Archway.
Then you take me to Scotland Yard.

MARTIN *{to John}*:
I'm glad I remembered something.
To tell the truth,
A moment ago, when the officer asked me,
I couldn't remember my own address.

I don't know where or who or what I am.

FINIS

IV

Recent Work

Memorial

We spoke, we chose to speak of war and strife—
    A task a fine ambition sought—
And some might say, who shared our work, our life:
    That praise was dearly bought.

Drivers, interpreters, these were our friends.
    These we loved. These we were trusted by.
The shocked hand wipes the blood across the lens.
    The lens looks to the sky.

Most died by mischance. Some seemed honour-bound
    To take the lonely, peerless track
Conceiving danger as a testing-ground
    To which they must go back

Till the dry tongue fell silent and they crossed
    Beyond the realm of time and fear.
Death waved them through the checkpoint. They were lost.
    All have their story here.

Yellow Tulips

Looking into the vase, into the calyx, into the water drop,
Looking into the throat of the flower, at the pollen stain,
I can see the ambush love sprung once in the summery wood.
I can see the casualties where they lay, till they set forth again.

I can see the lips, parted first in surprise, parted in desire,
Smile now as a silence falls on the yellow-dappled ride
For each thinks the other can hear each receding thought
On each receding tide.

They have come out of the wood now. They are skirting the fields
Between the tall wheat and the hedge, on the unploughed strips,
And they believe anyone who saw them would know
Every secret of their limbs and of their lips,

As if, like creatures of legend, they had come down out of the mist
Back to their native city, and stood in the square,
And they were seen to be marked at the throat with a certain sign
Whose meaning all could share.

———

These flowers came from a shop. Really they looked nothing much
Till they opened as if in surprise at the heat of this hotel.
Then the surprise turned to a shout, and the girl said, "Shall I
    chuck them now
Or give them one more day? They've not lasted so well."

"Oh give them one more day. They've lasted well enough.
They've lasted as love lasts, which is longer than most maintain.
Look at the sign it has left here at the throat of the flower
And on your tablecloth—look at the pollen stain."

Martine's Song

Write a letter to the dead.
Write it for the dead to read.
Oh the dead have swum too far.
They have swum beyond the sea.

Take the letter in your hand.
Make a fold, and make a fold.
Make it into a little boat
And place a candle in the hold.

Let the paper boat float on
Where the river meets the sea.
That is where my heart belongs.
That is where I long to be.

Every candle is a star.
Every boat floats out to sea—
Which I think is not too far
And that is where I long to be.

And that is where I long to be.

Everything in Your Window Is a Sign

I'm at the intersection
Looking up at your place
And everything in your window seems a sign.
You've some important work to do
And your work is bugging you.
You're angry as you try to fix the blind.
She should have done that long ago.
I would have fixed that blind, I know.
I'll know what to do for you. I'll know it fine.
Everything in your window is a sign.

> Everything in your window is a sign.
> Everything in your window is a sign—
> The coffee cup, the plant, the screen—
> I know everything they mean.
> They mean: if I wait longer here, you're mine.
> Everything in your window is a sign.

I'm at the intersection
And it's already late
And people turn to look as they go by.
You're sitting up there at your screen
And I'm confident you've seen
You've a worshipper who's waiting at your shrine,
Someone with healing in her hands,
Someone who truly understands

How two lives can truly intertwine.
Everything in your window is a sign.

Everything in your window is a sign.
Everything in your window is a sign.
The angle of the blind, the light
Tell me what I sensed . . . is right.
I'm right. You're waiting up for me. You're mine.
Everything in the window is a sign.

We're at an intersection
And our lives are looking up
And everything is working by design.
You're going to tell her soon, sometime.
You're going to break the news, sometime.
But she's in bed. She thinks that you're on line.
She's going to think: what a fool I've been
All the time I've been with him—
I never asked myself: what's on his mind?
Everything in your window is a sign.

Everything in your window is a sign.
Everything in your window is a sign—
The way you frown at what you see,
The way you don't look down at me—
Look down at me, you don't look down on me . . .
Because you *know* I'm here, you *know* you're mine.
Everything in your window is a sign.

Was That Your Idea of Love?

Was that your idea of love?
Was that your idea of love?

Those brilliantly confected lies—
They hit me straight between the eyes.
Was that your idea of love?

That endless digging for the dirt,
That motive-seeking where it hurt—
Was that your idea of love?

And all those accusations you made
About the subtle ways you'd been betrayed—
Was that your idea of love?

It felt like drowning. It felt like an immersion
In a dark sea of blame
Until I found out that it was all a diversion.
You had a secret game.
You had a game to play and you played rough.
Was that your idea of love?

Funny I never noticed it creeping up on us,
This vengefulness and spite.
Funny how long I went on thinking
There must be a simple way to put things right.

And funniest of all to think of you
Pretending to seek professional advice,
When what you wanted was to be shot of me
At any cost to anyone,
At any price
To me . . .

Was that your idea of love?
Was that your idea of love?

Resentfulness disguised as charm,
That care in plotting future harm—
Was that your idea of love?

That skilful use of evidence
To get beyond each last defence—
Was that your idea of love?

That conjuring of bad from good,
That mimicry of victimhood—
Was that your idea of love?

You certainly deserve congratulation
On an effective campaign.
I'd like to know the terms for outright capitulation.
But I suppose you've made it plain
They're going to be tough.
Was that your idea of love?

Be shot of me I beg you. Let me be.
Tell me again you want no more of me.
Was that the reckoning?

Was that the sum?
Or is there more of this—
Is there more of this to come?

Is this your idea of love?
Is this your idea of love?

Be shot of me I beg you. Let me be.
Tell me again you want no more of me.

Is this your idea of love?

The Alibi

My mind was racing.
It was some years from now.
We were together again in our old flat.
You were admiring yourself adjusting your hat.
"Oh of course I was mad then," you said with a forgiving smile,
"Something snapped in me and I was mad for a while."

But this madness of yours disgusted me,
This alibi,
This gorgeous madness like a tinkling sleigh,
It carried you away
Snug in your fur, snug in your muff and cape.
You made your escape
Through the night, over the dry powdery snow.
I watched you go.

Truly the mad deserve our sympathy.
And you were driven mad you said by me
And then you drove away
The cushions and the furs piled high,
Snug with your madness alibi,
Injured and forgiven on your loaded sleigh.

I Kept That Gun

I kept that gun you gave me.
It's up there still—on the shelf.
I kept that beautiful gun you gave me.
I thought one day I'd use it on myself.
Anyway
It's as you used to say:
It was something
To remind me of you.
I kept that gun you gave me
And I kept those bullets too.

I kept those bullets you gave me.
I've saved them up—all this time.
I kept those beautiful bullets you gave me.
I thought one day I might need them for some crime.
Anyway
It's as you used to say:
You'll only know you need it
When the deed is done.
I kept those bullets you gave me.
I kept them there—in that gun.

> Nice of you to drop by again unannounced
> Now that you're at loose ends.
> Nice of you to drop by again
> And suggest we could still be friends.

And it's a nice thought
That it's never too late
To make up
Though sometimes it might be too soon.
Who was it put that thought in your head
And gave that thought that tune?

I kept that wound you gave me.
I kept it here—in my heart.
I kept that beautiful wound you gave me.
When you tore my life apart.
Anyway
It's as I used to say:
That wound
Would remind me of you.
I kept that wound you gave me
When you informed me we were through—

When you told me you had somebody else
And how you felt this time she was truly the one.
Sit down and let me fix you something.
I'm glad you came—
I'm glad to find you're just the same—
And I'm glad, glad, glad—
I'm glad I kept that gun.

Down to the Twigs and Seeds

"The unexamined life is not worth living,"
As Socrates or someone somewhere said,
And I support that view without misgiving.
I can't get out of bed.
I reach out for the ancient herbal preparation
Known to the likes of Socrates as pot.
Oh yes, this life of mine requires examination.
For instance, I remember now,
That I forgot
That
I'm

Down to the twigs and seeds,
Down to the twigs and seeds—
I'm feeling rough,
I need a puff
But I'm down to the twigs and seeds.

    Where's a guy to go in the evening?
    Where's a guy to go at night?
    Where's a guy to find understanding
    When he's feeling far from bright?
    Everybody's got my number.
    Everybody's out of town.
    No one's picking up the receiver

And all the blinds are down,
Down, down to the . . .

Down to the heart that bleeds,
Down to the fundamental needs—
I'm out of cash,
I've smoked my stash
And I'm down to the twigs and seeds.

Where's a guy to find fulfilment?
Where's a guy to find release?
Where's a guy to find a filter?
Where's a guy to find some peace (of mind)?
Everybody's at the movies.
Everybody's gone to church.
How's about that for selfish?
Leaving all the junkies in the lurch!
I'm lurching . . .

Down to the twigs and seeds.
Down to the twigs and seeds.
Hello, it's me.
It's an emergency!
'Cos I'm down to the twigs,
Down to the twigs,
Down to the twigs and seeds!

Never Let Me See You Suffer

I hate a hot hard-boiled egg
But I adore a cold one.
I hate a brand-new pair of expensive shoes
But I love a comfy old one.
I hate my favourite thing
The way it shouldn't be.
I hate the thought of you unhappy.
Just keep all that crappiness away from me.

Never let me see you suffer.
Never let me see you blue.
Never let me see you strapped to the buffer.
Never let me see the train run into you.
Lie to me.
Don't cry to me.
Put on a cheerful smile.
Never let me see you suffer, baby
Or I'll run a mile.

Some say this attitude is immature.
Indeed, it's hard to defend it.
I like a passion to be plain and pure
And if it's not—I like to end it.
I like a prettily mascaraed face
With plenty of powder and lipstick

But when the makeup runs all over the place
That's the time I check the dipstick.

Never let me hear you weeping.
Never let me hear you sob.
Never let me hear you come home creeping
With your hanky in a big wet blob.
Throttle it.
Just bottle it.
Stifle all your inmost fears.
Never let me hear you weeping, baby
Or I'll disappear.

I like a woman with a magic glow.
Does that deserve a stricture?
I like a woman for the outward show
And not the inward horror picture.
If your psychology's a dreadful mess—
If there's that fly in the ointment—
Then my apologies 'cos I've a press-
ing appointment.

Never let me catch you thinking.
Never let me know you're down.
Never let me feel my senses sinking
When the buzz is you are back in town.
Life and soul!
Be my *wife* and soul
But never be a bit depressed.
Never let me see you suffer, baby
Or I'll flit the nest!